FATHER KNOWS LESS

LESSONS I LEARNED FROM MY KIDS

LEE KALCHEIM

Copyright © Lee Kalcheim 2014

All rights reserved, including the right of reproduction in whole or part in any form. For information, address Julia Lord Literary Management, 38 W Ninth St, New York, NY 10011.

This book is a work of fiction. Names, characters, places, and incidents either are products of the author's imagination or are used fictitiously. Any resemblance to actual events or locales or persons, living or dead, is entirely coincidental.

Print ISBN: 978-0-7867-5582-0
ebook ISBN: 978-0-7867-5583-7

Distributed by Argo Navis Author Services

To Julia, Samuel and Gabriel,
who made my life complete.

CONTENTS

1. TV OR NOT TV ... THAT IS THE QUESTION 11

2. HOW TO BE INSULTED AND NOT BE HURT BY IT 25

3. HOORAY FOR YOU KNOW WHAT 31

4. TRAVELING: GETTING AWAY FROM YOU KNOW WHERE. 43

5. RETURN TO LA LA LAND. 53

6. NO PENISES AT THE TABLE 67

7. HITLER'S BATHROOM 77

8. DAMNED YANKEES? 89

9. ROMAN (WORKING) HOLIDAY 99

10. THE BLUE GROTTO 109

11.	SKETCHES	117
12.	DIECI MINUTI	127
13.	THE HOOD	135
14.	THE LAST WORD	143
15.	THE "CLEVELAND RESPONSE"	151
16.	LETTING GO	161
17.	WAKE UP, MR. PRESIDENT	179
18.	YES, THERE IS A SANTA CLAUS	189
19.	SOOTHING THE SAVAGE BREAST	205
20.	DON'T TAKE IT PERSONALLY	219
21.	TEACHERS	229
22.	SEX, LOVE, AND MONEY	241
23.	THE GRAND (OR NOT SO GRAND) TOUR	251
24.	RENAISSANCE	265
25.	SEPARATION AGREEMENT	273

PREFACE

There's a story that may be apocryphal, attributed to Mark Twain. He notes, when he was sixteen, how stupid his father was, but when he was twenty-one, he was amazed how smart his father had become in the ensuing five years.

What has occurred to me, as my twin boys move through Twain's know-it-all years and head toward enlightenment, is that I think I have learned a great deal more from them then they ever learned from me.

(A scene from the original pilot script for the TV series, *Dadoo* later titled *Something Wilder* on NBC when Gene Wilder took the lead role.)

GENE'S HOME.

(Gene as "Dadoo" sits rocking his twin boys. "Dadoo" is the name the boys called me. It was the second word they spoke after "cat." So from then on I was "Dadoo." Still am. Gene, as "Dadoo" looks up at the camera.

DADOO

I'm just trying to get my boys to fall asleep. They woke me up, so until I get them back to sleep, I can't sleep. (sighs) I'm exhausted. I'm not their grandfather. I'm their father. Y'see I got married when I was forty-nine. My wife and I had twin boys when I was fifty two. (rocks them) Why did I wait so long? I used to play a game when I rode the subway. I look across and see four or five women, sitting opposite me. I'd pretend that I had to choose one. For life. Once I rejected one, I couldn't go back. If I kept rejecting then I'd have to choose the last one. Nine times out of ten I'd go all the way to the end, having rejected them all, and find that the last one was not nearly as attractive as the first. Or the third. It was my life in microcosm. Now, mind you, I did not choose women solely based on their looks. This was just a subway game. But in some way, I suppose, I had been playing it all my life. So you can imagine how lucky I feel that I finally chose someone terrific. Who then gave me twin boys. (he thinks) I mean, if I had married my high school sweetheart Judy Riffleman, my children would now be thirty and I'd be a grandfather ... rocking to sleep a couple of two-year-olds. So big deal. Everything worked out perfectly. For me. I don't know about Judy Riffleman.

CHAPTER ONE

TV OR NOT TV ...
THAT IS THE QUESTION

When my twin boys were four years old, I got my own television series on the air. I hold my children directly responsible.

Before then, I had had a somewhat successful television writing career. I had won an Emmy writing for *All in The Family*. I had written episodes of *The Odd Couple* and *Sanford and Son*, and I even once wrote one for a clunker called *The Bobby Sherman Show* which was so torturous to write that I came down with a 102-degree fever. I also wrote scads of pilots. The only one ever filmed was called *Zero Intelligence* about a military outpost near the arctic circle. It never made it on air. It shouldn't have. I got fired before the pilot was shot. The rewrites were so awful that I was then called back in to rewrite the rewrites. Didn't help. But I got a taste of the grinder that you get put through when a show even gets close to going on the air. And then I forgot about it.

I got married and had twins and forgot about it. I went back to writing plays and interesting screenplays filled with complicated characters that elicited the same basic response, "We love Lee's writing, but this is not for us." Of course it's not for you—you're doing Terminator VII!

I had not given up the idea of trying to get a television series on the air; it's just that it was inconvenient. First of all, I didn't live in L.A. Some years back I'd gone to a wedding there, filled with studio execs and a non-minister minister who talked like a marriage counselor on Quaaludes, "This partnership is more than a commitment. It is a star-crossed binding of two impassioned souls." Okaaay. But at all the tables during the reception, the studio execs were making deals! Oh, I thought, " *I don't go to enough L.A. weddings to get ahead in this business.*

Second, I was *exhausted.* I had started fatherhood at fifty one. Though I was blessed with the desire to write and I was full of ideas, my chief idea was how to find time to *nap.* I cheated. I invented games I could play with my boys while *lying down.* There was no excuse for my exhaustion. After all, Julia was doing all the breast-feeding. I would've liked to have helped but ... I was no sloth. I got up every other morning on early patrol and played with the kids until the sun came up. I rocked them to sleep my share of the time when they were teething. But how could *I* get more sleep? My "lying down games." My favorite was "Restaurant!" I loved this game. I loved it because I could play it while I lay on the day bed, half asleep, and the boys would come up to me in little striped aprons, holding a little pad and they'd take orders from me for my meal. I sleepily listed the food I wanted for lunch ... and they'd toddle off to their play kitchen and whip it up and bring back a tray filled with various pieces of plastic representing grilled cheese sandwiches, soup, and chocolate cake.

My talent came to full fruition that year as I came up with an endless list of games that could be played with my kids while I was half asleep. "Hospital!" I was the patient, and as I lay in a coma they attended to me doing everything from listening to my heartbeat through a stethoscope (buy your kids a real stethoscope—it is the best toy ever!) to performing major operations. I stuffed pillows and teddy bears and baseball hats under my pajamas, and my brilliant team of surgeons cut them out. "When did I swallow that Teddy Bear, I don't remember that?" And when one child woke up first, I could play "Airplane" with him. He'd sit on my stomach and I held up my hands, thumbs out for the control stick and he'd fly the plane—me—as I rolled and twisted and bounced. All with my *eyes closed*.

My other favorite thing was to read to them at night. I even read some of the same books I'd had read to me when I was kid, way back during the Roosevelt administration. And sometimes I'd lie with one of them when he had trouble sleeping and listen to a baseball game, the quiet, comforting drone of the announcer putting us both to sleep, until a sudden rally woke me. One night, lying next to Gabe, listening to the soporific sound of an extra inning Mets game, I realized that I had become my father and Gabe ... me. Fifty years before, I had cuddled next to my dad, listening to the same seductive noise of the play by play. The circle of life touched me. I found myself getting teary at the thought. I was in heaven!

I realized that this was something I wanted to write about. And because I generally wrote comedy, there must be something funny about this. It's the writer's curse. You're feeling something intensely, and then suddenly you're pulled away from your experience and you start analyzing it. It stinks. It really does. You never fully experience anything because part of you is always recording it as it happens. And yet you do examine it, maybe, more fully than "civilians." And once you commit to writing about it, you get to relive the experience endlessly. Not a bad deal.

I wrote a monologue. A monologue about how, having waited so long to have kids, it was so intensely satisfying. I was an older dad, having spent so much time avoiding being one because ... well, I just didn't wanna grow up. Or at least grow old. And being a dad meant ... well ... being middle aged. I was beyond middle age. I was over fifty now. (It was still *called* middle age because the super optimists who define those terms figured that life expectancy was bound to reach 100 any day.) I was an older dad. I was not a hot property in the TV world. I had had two successful plays running in New York within two years. But that was ten years before. I was, for all intents and purposes, a dad! I'd saved my money from my halcyon days, and we were getting by. So I suppose I could just indulge in nothing but being a father. And realizing how lucky I was, I wrote a monologue. And then this scene, about taking the boys to their first day at day care, creating a fictional Bill and Annie and Nate and Hal for me and Julia the boys.

INT. BOYS BEDROOM—NIGHT

(Bill is in his pajamas. He kisses the sleeping boys. He stops. He looks longingly at them and then turns to the camera.)

     BILL (to camera)

There's nothing as beautiful as a sleeping child. Especially when you haven't made love to your wife for a week.

(He moves off to his bedroom.)

INT. BEDROOM-NIGHT

(Bill enters in his Pajamas. Annie is in bed. He gets into bed.)

BILL

Honey? The kids are asleep. (He listens.) Yes. They are. Maybe we could ... (nuzzles her)

ANNIE

Bill, I'm not in the mood.

BILL

Well, hell I'm not in the mood either, but both kids are asleep. We don't get this chance very often. Nate's gonna want a drink of water in a minute. Let's get in a quickee.

ANNIE

I'm not interested in a quickie.

BILL

OK, we'll do a "longie." If Nate cries we'll just concentrate. We won't hear it. It'll be—

ANNIE (sits up)

Do you know what Monday is?

BILL

Monday. Monnnnnnday issssss …

ANNIE

Monday is the first day of *school!*

BILL

School? They're only three.

ANNIE

Preschool

BILL

Oh preschool. When I was a kid it was called nursery school. That sounds too childish today. God forbid a child should go to a place that sounds childish!

ANNIE

You're being insensitive.

BILL

When? Where? Let's back this up. I'll start again by asking if you want to make love and when I say the insensitive thing, you hold up your hand OK? The kids are asleep. How about if we …

(Annie holds up her hand)

BILL

What did I say??

ANNIE

I'm *worried* about them. I'm *worried* about preschool and *you're* making light of it!

BILL

I'm not making *light* of it. I'm making *nothing* of it. It's nothing.

ANNIE

It's their first day of *school*. It's *different* from play dates with friends. There's more at stake. It's more competitive. The kids may be smarter, quicker, more sophisticated. Our boys may be in over their heads.

BILL

They're not going to Harvard!

ANNIE

You don't understand.

BILL

What don't I understand?

ANNIE

You play with them at home. You, you, you wrestle with them, you, you …

BILL

Paint …

ANNIE

Paint with them. You tell them wonderful stories. You cook pancakes and cup cakes and …

BILL

Stir fry.

ANNIE

Stir fry with them, but you don't… I'm not criticizing you, I'm just telling you that you don't see them much with *other* kids. You know them from just playing with *you*. They're different from other kids.

BILL

Different how? What? Funnier? Nuttier? They probably know more "knock knock" jokes than other kids.

ANNIE

They're more *innocent* than other kids.

BILL

Innocent?

ANNIE

Innocent. Sheltered. Naive, sweet, vulnerable. (She turns away and cries.)

BILL

Honey ...

ANNIE

We've been too selfish. We've smothered them with affection. Instead of rushing home for lunch so you could roll around on the floor with them, you should have been toughening them up.

BILL

Toughening them up? Like what? Taking them on a canoe trip without rations?

ANNIE

Street tough. Life tough. They're gonna get *killed* in preschool.

(She cries again. Bill holds her.)

BILL

Honey. Honey. They're gonna be fine. Just fine. Look, there's no such thing as loving a child too much. Loving a child gives him confidence. When a child has confidence, he can deal with *anything*.

ANNIE (through tears)

I wish I had confidence that *they* had confidence.

BILL

Well, let me make love to you. It'll give you confidence.

(Bill pulls her down to him and kisses her. We hear off:)

HAL (O.S.)

Dadoooo. I want a drink of water!

(Bill stops kissing. Gets up. Starts out. Turns to Annie)

BILL

Save my place.

HAL (O.S.)

Dadooo!

(Bill reluctantly leaves the bedroom to answer his
on's call)

Writing this scene changed my life—only because what really changed my life was finding a fabulous woman and *having children*. As a young man, I was reluctant to get married. Too in love with my work. Raising a family would, I thought, distract me from what was important. But acknowledging Mr. Twain, when I was older, I realized how stupid that young man had been and that the love I had for writing was incomparable to the love I had for my family.

SCENE: THE. KITCHEN, FARMHOUSE, MASSACHUSETTS—NIGHT

(Lee and Julia are finishing their dinner. They hear one of the twin boys crying upstairs in his crib in the bedroom. Lee gets up).

LEE

I'll go.

(He is up, out of the kitchen, and trudging up the narrow stairs toward the crying boy.)

SCENE: THE TWINS ROOM—NIGHT

(Lee enters and moves to Gabriel, who is standing in his crib, crying)

LEE

I'm here kiddo. Dadoo's here!

(He moves to Gabriel, his arms outstretched to pick him up.)

LEE

Dadoo's here.

(About to pick him, up Gabriel screams)

GABE

No! I want Mommy!

(Thrown by this, Lee steps back. He thinks maybe Gabe will change his mind. He takes a step toward his son again.)

GABE

I want Mommy!

(He's got the message. He turns and stumbles down the stairs and into the kitchen)

SCENE: KITCHEN—NIGHT

(Julia looks up as he enters. We hear the baby still crying. Julia looks at him)

LEE

He wants his sainted mother.

CHAPTER TWO

HOW TO BE INSULTED AND NOT BE HURT BY IT

This was not a made-up scene. This happened, and I was crushed. I'd just been rejected by a one-and-a-half-year-old. "What's wrong with me?" I wanted to ask him. I wanted to shout out: "I'm partly responsible for your very existence. It was I who traipsed up to the hospital every day to hold your little finger after you had inhaled amniotic fluid and lay in the intensive neo-natal care unit, while your brother had come home with Mommy. When you were finally released, I was the one who wrapped your tiny body inside my coat and took you home on the subway because I couldn't find a cab. Your first subway ride was with me! Your first gritty New York experience was with me, 'Dadoo!'

But you were having nothing to do with me, despite the fact that I was the one who stayed up nights so your exhausted mother could sleep after breast-feeding both of you all day. I stayed up all night and wrote, with your little crib sitting in my study, poised to heat your bottles as soon as you cried out. There I was, trying to write a sit-com episode at four in the morning, while you gurgled and wheezed and had not one single idea for a scene-ending punch line! I did all of this for you, and now you tell me, "I want Mommy!"

Sure, I wanted to rail against this injustice, but I called on every adult gene in my body and fortified myself against overreacting. I went to fetch his mother. And as I walked away, rejected, hurt, it suddenly occurred to me. Hell if I were him and I had a choice between a soft, blue-eyed woman whose warm breasts I could cuddle against, and drink from *or* a bony, mustachioed man with rough, carelessly shaven cheeks and *New York Times*-print-stained fingers, whom would I choose? Mommy, of course! This kid was no idiot. This kid was asking for what any red-blooded American male would want, if he had a choice. Why should I be insulted? If I'd had the guts when I was one and a half years old, I would have said the same thing to my father! Not only did this kid have the courage of his convictions, he had the courage of *my* convictions!

How many times had I been in situations where, faced with telling someone what I really wanted to say with the risk of hurting their feelings, I chickened out and told them what they wanted to hear and got, as my mother again would say, "bubkis" (nothing)?

They felt good. I did not get what I wanted, so I didn't feel good. What was the point? Why couldn't I say what I really wanted? I remember walking down the aisle about to marry my first wife. I was twenty seven. I thought, *I'm too young to die. What am I doing?* "I looked around at the crowd. I can't renege. All the people who sent us gifts, who came to the wedding. What would they think? What would *they* think? Would they have thought ill of me if I had shouted, "I want my mommy!"?

I remember once working on a TV pilot script with a producer

I'd just met. We were riding in a cab, back from lunch, and he leaned over and said to me, "Y'know, I can tell we're gonna be friends. Really good friends." At that moment I thought, *Who says that kind of thing?* I knew right then and there that this relationship was doomed. I was going to get screwed. Friendships are built over many years and many shared experiences. He knew from one lunch? I mean, if I had just turned to him and said,

NO! I WANT MOMMY!

"You're kidding!" maybe he would have greater respect for me and the work I did for him. Probably not. He didn't understand the nature of friendship. He certainly wouldn't have understood why I thought he was kidding. I do know I would've felt a helluva lot better.

Because the fact is, years after my first wife and I were divorced, I had lunch with her and she was very rational about the mistake that we had made. We were probably both aware of the rationalizations we were making to justify the marriage. She wanted to be married. I didn't know what the hell I wanted. And we did it. It ultimately caused no harm to either of us. We both remarried happily. But I didn't learn anything from not telling her the truth. I learned it from my little son, when *he told* me the truth. The truth hurts sometimes, but if you *think* beyond the pain, you learn something about yourself that is much more valuable than any flattering lie. I learned that the insult, "No, I want my mommy" was not an insult *if* I put myself in his place. Who wouldn't want to snuggle with his mommy? I do.

SCENE: WARNER BROTHERS, THE SET OF FRIENDS

(Gabriel is standing with his father, Lee, and the director, Michael Lembeck, as Jennifer Aniston walks over to Gabriel and kneels down in front of him.)

JEN

Hi. I'm Jen. Who are you?

GABE

Gabriel.

JEN

What a lovely name. Would ... would you like to see the set?

GABE

(Looking back to his dad to see if it's okay. Lee nods)

Sure. Thanks.

(Jennifer takes Gabriel's hand and walks off with him, hand in hand, as Lee and Michael watch)

                        MICHAEL

Nice couple.

                        LEE

Yes. She could do worse.

CHAPTER THREE

HOORAY FOR YOU KNOW WHAT

Why was I on the set of *Friends* at Warner Brothers? Because the little scene I wrote about Julia and the boys took me there. I had sent it off to my successful director friend Barnet Kellman, who was directing *Murphy Brown* in L.A. Barnet had directed one of my plays. He was a fine director. Smart and tough and patient. He'd finally left directing theatre and gone to L.A to try to make a decent living. I knew a few people out there. Gave him some names. He got some work. They found out he was good. He did some pilots. And hit it big with *Murphy Brown*. He told me he had resisted going to L.A., as most theatre people do at first. But once there, he found that "They don't treat you any more like shit than they do in the theatre and they pay a helluva lot more."

Barnet liked the stuff I wrote about the kids. My older dad musings. He gave me some notes. I worked on it. And next thing I know I'm in L.A., and we're reading the scenes (I'd expanded the scene into the whole first act of a series pilot) in a friend's living room with a pretty good cast, including Judd Hirsch and Jennifer Aniston.

It read pretty well. We decided to take it to the studio where he worked, Warners, and present them with a reading. We called Judd, but he wouldn't consider *reading* the scenes for studio executives. Call him when you had an offer. So I said to Barnet, "You know, I can read this part myself. I'm not great actor, but I can deliver it. And if *I* can make it work, they'll think, Imagine how good this would be with someone really good! We decided to take a shot. We assembled a group of actors and me in a conference room at Warners. Les Moonves and his staff listened.

They laughed. They did not rustle papers or take phone calls or doze. They seemed amused. A day or so later we were sitting in offices at NBC, where we were told, "We like this project. If you can find a star for it, we'll make a pilot."

We were overjoyed. Wait a minute! If *we* can find a star for it? Barnet and I looked at each other. "Isn't this *their* job?" "Aren't *they* the network?" "Aren't *they* supposed to get the star?" We decided, "Let's not quibble." This is all better than a "No." This is a qualified "Yes." If they don't like it enough to find the star themselves, but they like it enough to challenge *us* to find one, we shall rise to the challenge!

We consumed lists of actors. Then lists of actors that the network wanted to do business with. I'd never heard of most of them. Because I was exhausted from raising kids, I hadn't watched TV for the last three and half years. I noticed that two people were not on the list. Judd Hirsch and Bobby Sherman.

I went back to New York. To the family. I figured, well, like most things, this wasn't going to happen. Barnet went from our optimistic, "It's a qualified yes" to "You know if they really want to do something they don't tell you to get the star. It's a basically a 'runaround no.' But we'll go through the drill. We'll look." Barnet's agency handled Gene Wilder, so they sent the scenes off to Gene. Couldn't hurt. He'd just had a show on air the previous year that had tanked. They weren't serious. They wouldn't want to do another show with him. He wouldn't want to try again so soon. *Pro forma* runaround.

I was meeting a woman in New York who was a seer. Yes, a seer. She read palms and tarot cards and told your fortune. Why you may ask? To find out about my future? No. She had a television series idea! Of course. Who doesn't? As I was later to find out in L.A., our pool cleaner, our gardener, the checkout girl at Ralph's Supermarket, all had series ideas. Why was I meeting with this nutcase? Because, frankly, I needed the work. Maybe somehow, some way, she did have an interesting idea for the series. We met in the bar of a hotel lobby that had been flooded in a recent rainstorm. It smelled like the basement of our house in Massachusetts after the spring rains. The room had the same doomed feeling as the project. "What is your series idea about?" I asked her. She leaned to me intensely, taking my hand in her purple-nailed hand. "Me." "You?" "It's about a woman who can tell the future." Okay, I've got to stop here. You get a sense very quickly when you hear an idea that you know (a) you don't want to write and (b) if you do write, it will not ... will *never,* ever sell. But then, you figure, you know ... maybe, just maybe, she has a twist on this that is so unbelievable so charming, so funny, so ... new that it could be a series. I'm here. I'm having a beer in a mildew stinking bar, what else have I got to do? So, she told me what she does. She tells the future. And I start ruminating. Coming up with ways we could make that character the center of a series. I'm selling *her* on her own idea. And she loves it. Why not? Am I desperate or what? I check my watch. Oy, it's late. I lean to her:

"Uh ... before I go ... could I ask you to tell me something about my future?"

"Of course."

"Will my television show get on the air?"

She took my hand. Opened it. Looked intently. Moaned. Sighed. Then nodded.

"Yes," she said, "I see much success."

I decided to quit while I was ahead. I could have asked her to be more specific. She saw success in what? My garden would be successful this summer? My old Volvo would get us through another winter? What? Didn't ask. Took the news as good and said I was late for dinner. I was beat. I'd spent an hour and a half coming up with ideas for a TV series for a woman whose own idea I thought had absolutely no merit until I started coming up with my ideas for her. Wait a minute, you take a bad idea, but because you have nothing better to do, you convince yourself it's a good idea. Remember when Coca Cola came out with "New Coke"? Did anybody raise his hand and say, "Why are we doing this?" Ditto: Going into Vietnam, Iraq, etc., etc.

I called home to tell Julia I was on my way.

"Call Barnet. He's called four times!"

I called Barnet.

"Gene loves it! I'm flying to New York on the redeye. We're going to his house tomorrow. A limo will pick you up at noon!"

Son of a bitch. The seer was right. I fell down laughing.

The next day I was riding up to Gene's house with Barnet in a limo. I thought, *Okay, if nothing else happens, this is a giggle.* And I remembered another thought, a kind of shibboleth about the business: If anything's going to happen, it happens quickly. This was happening quickly. Of course it took Richard Attenborough twenty years to get *Gandhi* made. I wasn't making *Gandhi*. I was only making *Dadoo*. That's what we were calling the series. The name the boys had called me since they first learned to speak.

Gene was as Gene looks like he'd be—warm and charming and very responsive to the material. Interesting, because he'd never had children. But as we all know from his screen persona, particularly in *Willie Wonka and The Chocolate Factory,* he entranced children by communicating a silly, fetching, off-beat, childlike quality of his own. We talked about the scenes. What we wanted to do. What he wanted to see. And we noticed he had a tennis court. So we talked about tennis.

And things did indeed happen quickly. Warners committed to making a pilot. Jennifer Grey was cast as Gene's wife, and auditions were held to cast the roles of Sam and Gabe. You don't know weirdness until you go to a casting call and see dozens of young boys auditioning to play the part of *your* boys. Gene came in to meet all the kids, and Julia stopped by with Sam and Gabe to say hello to Barnet when we took a lunch break. Gene came over to greet them and pointed out that Gabriel, with his auburn hair and big eyes looked just like him as a young boy. "He *could* be my son." Then Sam, with his booming foghorn voice, asked, "When are we going to eat?" Gene turned, "A great voice." Then turned to Barnet, "A great voice!" Julia felt a chill. Nope. Her kids were *not* going to be actors. At least not now. And she was not going to be a stage mother. She pulled them both to their feet and, giving a big hug to Barnet and sweet smile to Gene, said, "Boys are starved. Good luck today!" And whisked them off and out of show business.

We ended up with two terrific kids from Los Angeles that we saw on tape. We had our cast. And what seemed like a week later, but was probably a month, Julia and I and the boys were ensconced at the Oakwood Apartments in "The Valley" in L.A., shooting the pilot. Poolside at the Oakwood apartments was bizarre. During pilot season actors descend on L.A. to audition. We must not have been the only pilot with kids in the cast. There were at least a dozen other kids around the pool, sitting with their moms, who were holding scripts as they intensely went over their lines

"No, Allison, it's I *hate* this dress. Not, I hate this *dress.*"

Sam and Gabe sat in the shallow end of the pool with Julia while she read them *Winnie the Pooh*. I glanced over at them and thought, *right choice* and then went back to work "punching up" my pilot script.

I'd been away from manic TV writing for years, and suddenly I was being told that each scene had to end on a boffo line. When I wrote for *All In The Family,* Norman Lear's chief concern was always content, not laughs. I remember him once walking into the room while I was doing a rewrite with the story editors, and he said, "Hold it gentlemen. Before we do any rewrites, I think we ought to discuss what this episode is about." He is one of a kind. Now, TV had become all about the jokes. There couldn't be a moment of air. Funny. Funny. Funny. I had always prided myself on the fact that, if you took all the characters names off the script, you could still tell who said each line, because they were so true to that character—no on else could possibly say them. Now I was sitting around the Oakwood's Pool on the weekend and going through the script line by line and saying, "Is this funny enough? Can he say something funnier?" It was my first clue of what was to come. I had conceived of a show that would focus on the tiny details of bringing up kids. The nuance of raising children. Well, a bumper sticker most fitting for L.A. would read, "Fuck Nuance!"

I trusted Barnet, and if he felt it needed punch, I'd damn well give it punch. I can do punch. But I remembered fondly the weeks of rehearsal on the play we did together, *Friends*. It was a comedy, albeit about a man who was suicidal. And not once did the idea of making a line funnier ever come up. Of course, we had two hours to play out the lives the characters in this play. We would see them in highly dramatic situations as well as comic ones. We had time to draw our audience in. Get to know our characters. Let them laugh at the idiosyncrasies of these two guys. One of my favorite moments in the play had been when Ron Silver, playing Mel, a down-on-his-luck cartoonist living in a cabin in Vermont, is telling his guest, his oldest buddy and now the Assistant U.S. Ambassador to the U.N. (Craig Nelson) about his problems with women.

MEL

Y'see the problem is ... I go to a restaurant. I see a woman at another table. I like her looks. I look at her. I fantasize about her in bed. With kids. In a vital, intense discussion over breakfast. Dancing. Running on the beach. Being deliriously in love. Then the girl in the restaurant bites her nails or something. And I say, "Oh, oh, nervous. Skittish. Pent-up anger. Lots of fights. Irrational." And I break up with her right there. I fall in love with women, marry them, and break up with them all without ever meeting. I'm hopeless. Completely hopeless.

Not a joke in the speech. Just pure character revelation. But it got laughs. As Barnet would say, a TV episode is a 22-minute two-act play. Everything is condensed. No time for nuance.

We jumped headlong into shooting the pilot. Other comedy writers were brought in to help punch up the punch ups. I'm not sure any of the newly inserted jokes made the show any better, but I had a helluva good time sitting around the writers room with three other funny guys throwing out punch lines. I saw the idea of a subtle show about parenting slipping away. But I remembered the adage of an old ex-agent of mine who used to yell at me as I walked down the hall, "Funny is money!"

After a week of rehearsal and mad rewrites upon rewrites, we were ready to shoot the pilot. Julia and the boys were sitting in the front row of the stadium seats inside the Warner soundstage. An out-of-work comedian was warming up the audience. There were many delays, and having run out of warm-up material and noticing that there was more than the usual amount of kids in the audience he said, "Okaaaay, how about a little quiz for all the kids up there? Okaaaay how many of you like music?" Hands shot up. "Okaaay let's see how many musical instruments you can name? Let's start with stringed instruments." Some little girl yelled out "Violin" "Right!" Another "Banjo." "Right!" A mother yelled "Cello". Right. A little boy yelled, "Piano" "Right!" Sam, in his four year old foghorn voice belted out, "Wrong!"

The comedian looked up to see Sam leaning over the front row. "Wrong? What's wrong with that? A piano is a stringed instrument." "No, it isn't," said Samuel. "It's a percussion instrument. It has strings but the strings are *struck* by the piano's hammers. It's percussion!" "Okaaaay," said the comedian, "Let's hear it for the smart kid in the front row. What's your name?"

"Samuel."

"Why are you here tonight Samuel?"

"My father wrote this."

"Really? Is he a writer?"

"Of course."

"Okaaaay. Does he also play piano?"

"No, my mommy does."

"What do you play?"

"Nothing yet. But I'd like to play the violin."

"A stringed instrument, right?"

"Ha!"

Hearing Samuel banter with the warm up guy, I knew the whole idea for the series was right. I wanted it to be a show about special kids. Kids whose preoccupations were not only sports and toys and fast food and trips to Disneyland, but the myriad surprising things in life.

The pilot went reasonably well. The audience laughed. Gene was charming. The network execs wrung their hands. When I asked Gabriel, the critic, what he thought, he said, "OK, except the set doesn't look like our house. It's too neat."

After the show was shot, edited, and retitled *Something Wilder*, "real folks" were brought to a little studio for a screening. They were seated in special chairs with "reaction knobs" in the arm rests. They were shown the pilot and asked to press knobs when they "liked" or "disliked" what was going on on the screen. My TV future was in their hands. Literally in their hands.

I didn't want to wait around in L.A. for the results of the

screenings or for the network to make its decision. It would be at least another three, four weeks. I didn't want to sit around anywhere. I had some money now. We flew to Europe. To Brussels and then to London. Where they spoke the King's English. Unpunched.

SCENE: A RESTAURANT IN PARIS THAT SPECIALIZES IN "MOULE ET FRITE"

(Four year olds, Samuel and Gabriel, and their parents are seated and have been handed menus.)

                    LEE

Why don't we just have their specialty—Moule?

                    GABE

What's a Moule?

                    LEE

It's a mussel.

                    GABE

A muscle of what?

                    LEE

Not *that* kind of muscle. It's a fish. It lives inside a shell.

SAM

What's a frite?

JULIA

A French fried potato.

SAM

The French don't call a French fry, a *French fry?*

GABE

That's silly.

JULIA

Well, frite means fried in French. And since we're in France, there's no need to identify it as French.

SAM

Okay.

GABE

What do the English call an English muffin?

CHAPTER FOUR

TRAVELING: GETTING AWAY FROM YOU KNOW WHERE

You would think that, if one wanted to get away from an anxious experience, one would go to a beach somewhere and just relax. Maybe even leave the kids with grandparents and just melt away. But I didn't need to relax in a way that would allow my brain to relive the intensity of the last month. I didn't want obscurely funny punch lines rolling around in my head. I didn't want to be wondering if the rewrites on the rewrites on the rewrites had been ... right. I didn't want to be wondering if the postal clerk from Encino who kept dozing at the screening was tired from watching an extra inning Dodger game or was bored to tears at *Something Wilder*. I wanted to be in another world.

We had friends in Brussels and London who had never seen the boys. And we wanted to show the boys to them and introduce Sam and Gabe to the world outside New York and Hollywood. A place that our civilization came from. We'd promised we'd take them to London, to Paddington station, where the great Paddington Bear was found and named and written about in one of their favorite books. That sealed the deal.

Friends cautioned us, "They're four. Their too young. The trip won't mean anything to them." "They're four going on forty," we said. "They'll get it."

But we forgot the "schlepping" part. Four-year-olds can't fly without car seats. Four year olds can't travel without strollers. Because we had twins, we had to take our double stroller. It's heavy! But we packed as economically as we could, making sure to include a collection of trains and planes and cars and stuffed animals for the boys. As the 747 rose up off the tarmac at JFK, the boys clutched their little Paddington bears to their chests, in their car seats, and Julia and I were too excited to even wonder if this was a good idea. It was a great idea.

Brussels. We stopped to see my old college friend and his wife, Tom and Irene, who lived in a house that had been an old inn—complete with a stream and a wonderful creaky old water wheel—the antithesis of Hollywood! They plied us with Belgian chocolates, and we slept in late, under our huge, downy bed covers. Then off we went to Austerlitz to see the battlefield where Napoleon had lost the battle of Waterloo. On the drive there I tried to fill the boys in on what little I knew about Napoleon.

"Well ... he was very short," I said.

"Is that good for a general?"

"Well, yes! It gave him an advantage over other generals because he was so short that they kept firing over his head. Never hit him!"

"Dadoo, didn't he sit up on a horse?"

"Yes. Yes, of course. And when you see paintings of him you'll see he always has one hand inside his jacket."

"Why?"

"Uh ... In an earlier battle. I think he lost a glove."

Fortunately at the battlefield, they had *real* information.

Rested and chocolated, we trained to Paris. Kids love trains, and these were *trains!* The TVGs. The long-nosed, sleek, super-fast pan-European trains. As the boys settled into their seats, they couldn't sit still.

"This train goes over a hundred miles an hour!"

"It does not."

"It does too."

"Who says so?"

"Dadoo told me."

"Dadoo's just joking. Dadoo always jokes."

"Mommy told me too."

"Oh, well ... maybe it's true."

The boys sat wide-eyed as the train pulled out of the station. The boys leaned over to each other every minute.

"How fast do you think we're going now?"

Gabe turned to me, "Dadoo, it doesn't seem very fast."

"Just you wait," I countered. Finally, past the outskirts of Brussels, the train accelerated . The scenery outside was a blur. Sam leaned to Gabe and whispered, "I think Dadoo was right. This is *really* fast." The respect I'd lost over Napoleon I gained back over the TGV!

In Paris, to our cabdriver's dismay, we piled all of our luggage, and the car seats, and the stroller into the pint sized Citroen. Surly, unhappy that he'd been burdened with American tourists and all of their worldly belongings, he grumbled as I sat in the front seat, forcing him to put his little leather pocketbook, his newspapers, and his carton of Galois on his lap. I instructed him in my best high school French where we were going. He stared at me as if I had addressed him Arabic.

"Pardon?"

"Nous voulons ... aller a la Hotel Saxe Residence."

"Saxe Residence? Non! Ou est la?"

"Uh ... a ... Neuf ... Villa de Saxe."

Gabriel spoke up from under the luggage stuffed around him in the back.

"Dadoo, are you trying to speak French?"

" I *am* speaking French."

"Maybe Mommy should try."

After much backing and filling and circling in the seventh *arrondisment,* we found the hotel, at the end of an alley. A charmingly quiet alley. With an elevator so small it took us seven separate trips to get all our luggage up to the room.

While the boys played with their train set on the bed in their room of a very small two room suite, we spread the Paris map out on the bed and planned our stay. The going was difficult. Well not difficult—just physically trying. We took only public transportation. What's more fun than a subway? The Metro. It's odd the details that fascinate kids.

"Mommy, Dadoo, these subways are so quiet."

"That's because their cars have rubber tires."

Gabe pondered this for a moment. He was used to the clackity-loud New York subways. "It's too quiet for a *subway*." Once inside the car, they showed a palpable thrill, as they squirmed into their seats. They loved riding the subway in New York. Sometimes they insisted we take one even if we were only going one stop away. And they would ride in the first car and look ahead at the track. On the Metro, they noticed that, when the doors were about to close, a funny horn sounded. And when you wanted to get out at your stop, you had to unlatch the door! These are great discoveries for a kid. There is no experience quite like unlatching your own subway door on a Paris Metro, stepping out into a spanking clean station, then turning to watch the cars ... move off silently into the tunnel. But carrying a double stroller up and down and up and down metro steps took its toll on my forearms. They ached. But we were glad to have the stroller when the guys began to wind down toward the end of the day. At the Musée D'Orsay, Gabe crawled into the stroller and slept, while Sam, with his last bit of energy, ran up and down the marble floors, sliding and laughing as he went. But they took it in. A few years later, when we were back in Paris, at the same museum, we "lost" Gabriel. And as I ran frantically back through the rooms of impressionist paintings, anxiously looking for him, I finally found him, just standing ... just standing and staring at a Renoir painting of a nude in dappled sunlight that both of us had said we'd liked when we'd seen it on that first trip. I just stood and watched him watching.

We don't know how much they "get." We just don't know. And when they give back, they give back like this—standing in front of painting that you both love, like a doctoral student studying it for his Ph.D., like a smitten young artist seeing Renoir for the first time, like a boy finding something he and his dad had fallen in love with and finds he is now able to gaze at again for as long as he wants, while his dad looks on, tingles going up his spine.

And on to London. Our friends in London, Jeanne and Dermott and their son Josh, lived in Peckham. Peckham is located in Southwest London. It is famous because, during the blitz, when the German planes were finished bombing central London and were flying back to Germany, to lighten their load, they dropped their unused bombs ... on Peckham.

It has recovered nicely, and its streets with rows of narrow cozy little houses are a bargain for Londoners in search of a home of their own at a reasonable price. Our friends own a lovely little house, and we were delighted to stay there—for several reasons. We got to see more of them. We got to sit in their garden for tea. And we got to take Brit Rail—the train—into central London!

"Here it comes. This one's going to Victoria Station. Who is Victoria station named after?"

"Queen Victoria!"

"No. It's named after Herbert J. Station!"

Requisite groans all around. The boys had heard that joke since they were toddlers as we crossed the Pulaski Skyway going to Philadelphia and I told them it was named after Herbert J. Skyway. Who was the Eiffel Tower named after boys?

"Herbert J. Tower !"

"Right!"

Energized by the half-hour train ride into London, the boys ran through Victoria Station to the street to gaze at the funny square-shaped taxi cabs and the double-decker buses. We crossed into the Royal Mews and on to Buckingham Palace.

"Jump in the stroller guys. We've got to hurry to get there for the changing of the guard."

"What do they change into?"

"They don't change into anything. They change."

"They change their underwear."

"Oh Mom-my!"

After the guards changed we crossed into Green Park and rolled down Piccadilly Street into Piccadilly Circus and down to Trafalgar Square. We pointed to the statue in the center of the square.

"That statue is of Admiral Nelson. He defeated Napoleon at the battle of Trafalgar."

"Napoleon lost *again*?"

"Yes, well ... his navy. And Nelson lost his life in the battle. Became a national hero. Now, look carefully at the statue. Notice something strange?"

"The pigeons really like it."

"Nelson only has one arm," I said, "He lost it at the battle of Santa Cruz. "

"Did they ever find it?"

"Boooooooooooooo!"

Long days at The National Gallery, a visit to Paddington Station to find the locker where Paddington Bear was found.

"How do you know it's this locker?"

"I remember from the book."

"It didn't say in the book we read."

"Yes, but Dadoo probably read an earlier version."

On to a boat trip up the Thames to Greenwich to see the *Cutty Sark* and the Clock Museum and then of course to … The Tower! We were aghast to find that the tour guide at the Tower loved scaring kids with all the grisly details of the untimely ends of famous Brits.

"After the rebellion, they cut off the 'eads of the conspirators and they put 'em all in a row along London Bridge … on top of long stakes … squishy side down!" I blanched. The boys didn't bat an eye. It was exciting. At the souvenir shop, we bought a pocket edition of the British Kings and Queens. An illustration of each monarch and brief description of his or her reign. Once the boys learned to read, they devoured it. They had been to the land that these rulers ruled. They'd heard tales of their cruelty and their cunning. They had seen the palace where, since the nineteenth century, they had lived in resplendent luxury. They had seen the tower where some had been consigned to ignoble fates. And by the time he was eight, Gabe had memorized the royal line and would, with some urging, proudly recite it and correct us if we faltered.

"No, Elizabeth did *not* succeed her father Henry the Eighth. First came his son, Edward the Sixth who died when he was twenty. Then came "Bloody Mary," a Catholic, who succumbed to cancer after spending her short reign beheading Protestants and *then* came Elizabeth. She was third in line, but ruled longer than anyone until Victoria."

"Yes, but was she *happy?*"

"Oh, Dadooo!"

All from a little book. From the souvenir shop. You never know.

We boarded the plane for New York. Not knowing if the show had been picked up. Or where we would be living. But I did know, I did learn that if you travel with your children—from the moment they are conscious that they are seeing something new and different, *you* will see something new and different, because you will see it all through their eyes.

"...SQUISHY SIDE DOWN!"

Message from Barnet Kellman on my answering machine when we got home:

BARNET

The good news is, the show's picked up. We're on the fall schedule. The bad news is we're on Saturday night at 8:00. When *no one's home*. But, if we can do better than expected, maybe they'll move us. Or maybe like *All in the Family*, we'll make people stay home on Saturday night to watch us. Oh, and the network wants to replace Gene's wife. And make a few other changes. They want the twins to be Siamese twins. Just kidding. How was London? You know the old joke, "Why did the Siamese Twins move to London? So the other one could drive." Ba dump bump! Come out ASAP. You'll need to rent a house. Congratulations. It's all uphill from here.

CHAPTER FIVE

RETURN TO LA LA LAND

Never rent a house from an ex-hippie, wealthy, Jewish weightlifter. Especially one with expensive tastes. What did I know? He was polite when he showed me the house. He was naked from the waist up, all the better to display his tattoo—a large Jewish star with the words "Never Again" scrolled beneath it. A political statement on his pect. His salt-and-pepper pony tail hung down his spine. He wore an earring. Small. Tasteful. He led me through the house, pointing out only the valuable things.

"This inlaid end table is the only one of its kind in the Western Hemisphere. This is a Navajo peace pipe. I smoke it once a year to honor my father's death."

"You're father was a Navajo?"

"No, he was a garment worker. He made shirts on Seventh Avenue."

"I see, then he was fond of Navajos?"

"He never met a Navajo. He was Jewish. He only knew Jews and the Puerto Rican boy who delivered lunch. He never made more than six thousand dollars a year. When he died I was making a million six."

I still didn't understand the Navajo connection, but my host plowed on.

"He left me two hundred and sixty dollars in his will. I bought the pipe with it."

I still didn't get it, but it didn't seem worth pursuing. He was on to the next object of value.

"This rug is worth fifty thousand dollars."

"Uhhh, maybe you should store that. We have four-year-old boys. They're very clean. Very neat, but they might spill something."

"No problem. It's a tough rug. It can take it."

"But ... "

"If you don't love these things, don't rent the house."

"I love them, I just don't want to hurt them."

"If you love them you won't hurt them."

Okaaay. Now what do I do? In his diffident hippie way he was saying, "It's all cool man. You love the house. It'll all be cool. Mi casa est su casa."

Fine, I thought. I can be cool. I hadn't really ever been cool. But if it meant renting this neat house, I could be cool. I rented it. A year later when we moved out, I had to go to small claims court because "Mr. Cool" had kept my deposit because he claimed my kids had drawn on his wall. Didn't touch his valuable rug. Or smoke his Navajo pipe. Drew on the wall. My kids never drew on the wall. In fact the spot where he pointed out some faint marks was too high for my kids to reach. They had never drawn on a wall in our Massachusetts house. Or New York apartment. Why would they do it in Mr. Cool's pristine house? In a spot they couldn't reach? Waiting to go to trial, we realized that we would have to wait half a day. We settled out of court. In the parking lot. And Mr. Cool kept enough of my money to buy another valuable knick knack for his home. No wonder he made a million six last year.

But before that happened, we indulged in the house. The master bed bathroom was larger than my first New York apartment. The walk-in closet was large enough not only to walk in, but to hold a decent sized party in. The living room had nothing but white couches in it. Perfect for four year olds.

"Not on the couch! No chocolate on the couch!"

And the pool was black. Everything in L.A. was black. The cars. The office furniture. The T-shirts under the leather jackets. Except us. We were white. And wet behind the ears.

Su casa est mi casa.

I had found a home away from home and called Julia and told her to pack up and come out.

"What's it like?"

"It's great. It's ... very L.A."

"Is that good or bad?"

"Well, if you're living here, you should get the feeling that you're really living *here*."

"But you don't really want to live there."

"Right, but since we have to live here, I thought, why not live here in a place that really reeks of *here*." If you can hear a double take over the phone, I heard Julia do one.

"Tell me something you love about the house."

"Uhhhh, well ... They have a rosemary bush. We can stuff chickens for a hundred years."

As it turned out, Julia and the boys loved the house. It was suitably funky. A black pool (of course). And a kumquat tree. If the show folded, we could always write *The Kumquat Cook Book*. Favorite recipe: Rosemary stuffed chicken with kumquat sauce. And it gave rise to family "knock knock" jokes.

"Knock Knock.

"Who's there?"

"Kumquat."

"Kumquat who?"

"I love you—kumquat may!"

Back in the land of "professional" comedy, Barnet and I met with network honchos to go over their notes on the pilot. The NBCers had read the questionnaires filled out at the screening replete with remarks such as: Love him hated her. Love her hated him. They need a dog. The friend isn't handsome enough. 86 the Friend. Etc. Etc. Based on both the audience survey and network sagacity, as Barnet had informed me, Gene's wife from the pilot was replaced by another actress. Because they wanted teenagers to watch the show, a teenage next-door neighbor was added as a regular character. Because they wanted "ethnic diversity," a black plumber was added for the new first episode. And even though the pilot was good enough for the network to order it for series, massive rewrites were demanded.

Because I drove to work every day, a strange phenomena for me—not driving, going to work every day, I bought a used convertible that seemed appropriately "Hollywood." Top down, I drove each morning to Warner Brothers, past the guard at the gate, top down, waving good morning, and feeling for all the world like Cary Grant in 1948. The best part of the day!

The show now had a staff. I don't know ... six, seven, eight writers. A head writer. A head writing team. They would run the show. Though the show was my creation, I'd never "run a show," so I would , with the lofty title of something like Associate Producer, simply be one of the staff writers. Understand that every writer on staff had a producer credit. At the top was Executive Producer. Then Associate Producer. Then Assistant Producer. All the way down to just "Producer." The titles meant nothing except they entitled them to a larger salary, since they were also now producers as well as writers, even though they weren't producing. When I worked on *All in The Family,* there was The Producer,

Norman Lear, and then there was everybody else. We in fact did *not* have a roomful of writers. There were two story editors. And then just plain old writers. Who worked at home and sent in the scripts when they finished them. I wrote most of my episodes from my beat up old desk in Connecticut. Pretty good show, considering. When my episode was shot, I flew out to L.A. and sat on the set like a playwright and did the rewrites needed. Alone. I could call in help from the story editors, if needed. With the *Something Wilder* staff, they never saw any rehearsals until the dress run-through. Notes were sent constantly up to the writers' room about what was not working. A mad rewrite was done on the basis of the notes and sent back down.

"The bedtime story scene with Gene and the boys isn't working. Charming but not funny."

"How about if he's had a garlic pasta for dinner and they can't stand his breath?"

"Garlic's always funny."

"I think Cosby did garlic with his son."

"Allergies!"

"What?"

"The boy's blankets were washed with a detergent that Gene is allergic to, and he keeps sneezing during the story."

"Gene can sneeze funny."

"Which is funnier, sneezing or garlic breath?"

"One of life's great questions!"

"Give him both!"

Not until that run-through did we see the show on its feet. And then, like herd of sheep, we moved *en masse* from one scene to the next. It was as if "the writer" was this seven headed monster. Working on *All in the Family* as I had worked in the theatre, I could sit on the set and watch and feel when something worked or didn't. Then tinker and adjust and find something better. Here, you had seven different writers, all with different takes, who were coming in to see it too late in the process. And, who after the network and studio execs got finished with their notes, were largely irrelevant to the process. Committees can't write plays. Even TV plays. The best TV shows have had the voice of one writer. *Seinfeld* was all filtered through the brain of Larry David. That's why all the characters sound like him. Have his New York, angst-ridden, insecure, warped view of life. And it works. David Kelly's shows, like 'em or not, are a product of David's brain. *Boston Legal* may be good one week and weak the next, but for the last minute or so alone, with James Spader and William Shatner just talking and smoking cigars on the office veranda, it is worth it. *West Wing* was worth it for the infusion of Aaron Sorkin's manic wit. The advent of the multi-staffed show (particularly with comedies) has homogenized the process. All the shows sound alike. They even have the same rhythm. Group writing (except for sketch humor, which is based on caricature, not character) just doesn't work. I often imagined what Arthur Miller would have had to put up with if *Death of a Salesman* had been staff written.

"Arthur, when Willy's wife says to his sons, "Attention... Attention must be paid to this man."

"Yes?"

"Well, it's a little heavy."

"She's not trying to be funny. She's trying to get her boys to show some respect to their father. He's in trouble. He needs their respect."

"I know. I know. Respect is good. But ... I mean ... Yes, Curt, what's your take?"

"How about, 'Come on kids, give dad a break.'"

"Too general. Yes, Sally?"

"How about... Dad's depressed. You know, a hug... a joke now and then..."

"Nooo, too on-the-nose."

"I think it's the word attention. It's so..."

"How about... just... 'Wake up guys! Dad needs some love!'"

"I like that. 'Wake up guys... Dad needs some love!' It's quick. It's direct. The word 'love' gets me more than the word attention. Attention is a downer word. What do you think, Arthur? Arthur? Where's Arthur?"

While I was in the writers' room rewriting dialogue that was projected from the computer onto a large screen in the room, Julia had to do full-time parenting. Thanks to old cereal boxes and her exquisite imagination, she produced a bevy of handmade toys. With scissors, glue, and Cheerios boxes she fashioned everything from airline pilot's hats to dueling swords. And after a weekend trip to San Francisco she asked the boys what they wanted to make next. "The Golden gate bridge!"

"Honey, I'm not sure we have enough used cereal boxes to make that."

"Mommy, you can do it."

"We'll empty out the full ones!"

It's amazing the things you can do that you don't think you could do because your kids just *know* you can do it.

Julia made the bridge. It spanned the entire length of the large glass coffee table. It was a wonder of pop art. Eat your heart out Red Grooms. When Barnet saw it at dinner, he sent the set decorator over to copy Julia's cereal box toys to use in the show.

Her finest creation came soon after. One Saturday evening we took the boys to the Hollywood bowl. I think more for the phenomenon than for the music. Sam and Gabe had never seen a classical music concert, and even if they became restless, we knew the setting itself would stimulate them. But that night, Izak Perlman was playing. And they were entranced. And when we got home, both of them said that they wanted to play the violin. The next day, Julia got out the scissors and, you guessed it, cut up cereal boxes and made two violins. Not just profiles of violins—cereal box violins worthy of Guarneri. With sound boxes and frets and strings made from rubber bands and chopsticks for bows. They gleefully held them up to their chins and sawed away, humming tunes as if, for all the world, they were Itzak at the Bowl.

Something Wilder premiered on a Saturday night in October. I wanted to be out of town. So, we all went up the coast to a funky old motel-resort north of Ventura. The San Diego to Seattle Amtrak train came right though the middle of the resort. We booked a little bungalow on a hillock over the ocean. At eight we watched the show. It was odd, to say the least, watching a show ostensibly about us, that had been rung through the rewrite wringer so many times that it could have been about a family from Mars. At 2:00 a.m. I woke the boys so that we could watch the train rumble through the resort on its way north. It came right on time, at 2:12, blaring its horn, and we all screamed and waved and watched it disappear down the track toward San Francisco. Gabe turned to us.

"That was better than the show."

The other shows, the new shows premiering with *Something Wilder* were big hits. *Friends. ER.* And the network decided they wanted, needed, to bolster that audience. *Dadoo,* i.e. *Something Wilder* had been designed as a "family show." But young adults were watching *Friends.* They wanted young adults, i.e. single men and women who wanted to watch other single men and women spend their time trying to hook up with other single men and women—so they changed *Something Wilder* into a show about a married couple, who *acted* like they were single. Huh? After the first few episodes, the kids all but disappeared. (Along with the teenager next door and the black plumber). It was now about this "hot" couple who kept getting involved in absurd dilemmas. Donald Trump's then-wife Marla Maples did an episode playing a vamp who tries to seduce Gene on a camping trip. The new wife, now played by Hillary Bailey Smith—a consummate comedian—was a great partner for Gene. But a show that suited the new premise should have been conceived for them. A kind of updated *Thin Man.* A sophisticated, tippling, high-living husband and wife in the fast lane. This show had one foot in the old premise—older Dad trying to raise kids—and one in the new—zippy couple getting into trouble. As charming as Gene was, as dexterous as Hillary was, the ship was sinking in its own contradictions.

It morphed into a kind of a sex farce. Years ago the British made a series of sex farce movies, *Carry on Nurse, Carry on Sergeant.* They'd take a milieu and people it with inept characters, busty women, double entendres and stupid chases, and—it's a laugh riot. Our show became a kind of *Carry On Dadoo.*

It had started with me writing a sweet scene about the lovely little things we go through bringing up our children. It was my life. And it somehow became a television series. Except ... my life had been rewritten.

F ... nuance.

A lot of shit hit a lot of fans during this year, and I ended up actually being fired from my own show. I was still on the payroll, but my input on the show was no longer welcome. But, I learned something wonderful from my wife. And from my kids. First, take the money and run. Perhaps money can't buy happiness, but it can buy freedom. With all the free time I had, I wrote a play. And the play was done that summer at The Williamstown Theatre Festival. And it was an exhilarating experience. And twelve years later, the play was expanded and produced again and done in Tokyo, Japan. Another exhilarating experience. But ... but, *more important,* had I not written another word that year, I was able to spend an enormous amount of time with my family. There's the old cliché that goes, "No successful businessman ever looks back on his life and says, 'I only wish I got to spend less time with my kids.' Most of the people I saw in Hollywood worked hard.

Really hard. And they didn't see much of their families. They didn't see their four-year-olds build a replica of the Golden Gate Bridge out of cereal boxes. They didn't get to go to the Hollywood Bowl to see Itzak Perlman and then have their boys decide on the spot that they wanted to play the violin. They didn't take them bike riding along the beach in midweek, when it wasn't crowded. They didn't lie on the floor with them in the middle of the day, on an old Navajo rug, and play "Ha"—a game where you put your heads on each other's stomachs and keep saying "Ha" in order, until one of you bursts out laughing and is eliminated. We were very lucky. It was all a game of "Ha."

I'd been eliminated from my own show. But I was laughing now on the floor with my family. They taught me it was all right. They were proud of me. That's it. They were proud of what I'd done. It didn't matter that the show wasn't what it should have been. Not to them. They were proud of me. And let me know it. And it got me through it all. As Arthur Miller said:

"Attention. Attention must be paid."

SCENE: THE PATIO OF A RENTED HOUSE
IN STUDIO CITY, CALIFORNIA.

(Samuel and Gabriel are sitting under a large sheet draped over a rosemary bush—a place they call "Rosemary House." They are pretending it is the cockpit of a 747. They are naked, as is their habit on a warm day in California. But they do wear pilot's hats, fashioned by their mother out of Rice Krispies boxes. Julia comes outside to call them in.)

JULIA

Sam, Gabe, Dadoo says that Jack Lemmon is coming for lunch. You have to get dressed.

SAM

Why?

GABE

We always eat without our clothes on.

JULIA

Not today. Not for Jack Lemmon.

SAM

Why? He's never seen a naked boy?

JULIA

It's not so much that you're naked, Sam, it's just that you tend to stand up on your chair and your penis is hanging over your plate. It's not … appetizing.

SAM

I won't stand on my chair.

GABE

He'll sit. Sam, you'll sit, okay?

SAM

Okay.

JULIA

Okay, but just in case, you have to wear shorts.

SAM

Oookay.

                    GABE

Okay.

(Gabe knits his brow. Thinking)

Mom?

                    JULIA

Yes?

                    GABE

Who's Jack Lemmon??

CHAPTER SIX

NO PENISES AT THE TABLE

It was bizarre! Even though my services were no longer needed for the series, finished scripts for each week's episode would be delivered to the house every Thursday morning. They were saying, "You're still on the team. But stay in the locker room." A check for said services would arrive in the mailbox on Thursday afternoon. On Friday evening I went to the filming of the show and watched a company of consummate actors play out a farce—an echo of something I'd once had in mind.

I got used to it—the way you get used to a beloved pet dying. It gnaws at you, but it doesn't take over your life. The job of a writer is to write. And so I kept writing. Other things. The house was leased until May, so while in L.A. I fashioned other series ideas (Hope springs eternal) and worked on the rewrite of a screenplay about a grandfather and his grandson on a road trip across the U.S. The old man has Alzheimer's and his dying wish is that he meet the old Hollywood star, Alice Faye, whom he once invited to his college prom. She refused with a lovely note, and ever since he has been dying to meet her. His grandson fixes up grandpa's old Indian motorcycle, and off they go to L.A.

Jack Lemmon had taken to the script and he was coming over for lunch to read through some scenes and discuss it... after Julia's admonitions that the boys must wear shorts at the table. We'd had guests for meals before, and the boys' nakedness at the table seemed more charming than off-putting, until one somewhat conservative couple, who not unsurprisingly had no children of their own, thought that nakedness had its place—but not at the dinner table.

"Yes, I explained, but we compensate by always going to bed fully dressed."

We weren't going to take any chances with offending Jack. After all, it wasn't a social visit. It was business. And as Oscar Wilde once said, "Nudity and business should never mix." The boys wore shorts. I explained to the boys who he was, and soon after his cream-colored Rolls Royce pulled into our driveway.

He was ebullient and charming. As energetic as Ensign Pulver in *Mr. Roberts*, as quirky as "Daphne" in *Some Like it Hot*, and as sweet as "Bud" Baxter in *The Apartment*. Julia made some croques monsieurs for lunch. Samuel piped up.

"They're French. We ate them in Paris."

"You were in Paris?"

"Yes! We also ate moule e frites"

"They call french fries, frites. Isn't that silly?" added Gabe. Jack widened his eyes and screwed up his face and said, in his best "Daphne" voice,

"The silliest thing I ever heard."

After lunch, Jack and I read some scenes and chatted, and when he left, I told the boys that we'd watch *Some Like It Hot* some day soon. It became the boys' favorite movie. They saw it so often they almost memorized it. And there was nothing as silly and fetching as Gabe's imitation of Marilyn Monroe singing in her breathy-sexy voice, "I Wanna Be Loved by You."

Soon after that meeting, friends out from back east came to visit for Thanksgiving—one of my oldest friends, Danny, and his wife, Freke, and young daughter, Samara. While Julia did the Universal tour with the girls and the twins, I took Danny for lunch on Sunset Boulevard for a glimpse of the Hollywood scene. We sat an overpriced outdoor café and reminisced about our first meeting, on a game show in New York called *Let's Play Post Office,* where fictitious letters from famous people were revealed line by line to the contestant, as they tried to guess who wrote them. We wrote the letters, filled with funny clues and usually ending with a pun on the celebrity's name. Dan wrote one for Ernest Hemingway, pleading with his tailor to make him pants with wide belt loops because he was a man "for whom the belt holes" were famous. (*For Whom The Bell Tolls*?) (Groan) And I ended the Robert Kennedy letter about a touch football game refereed by an incompetent woman named Kay with, "So, what are we going to do about our ref Kay? (RFK?) (Groan) No job we'd had since was as much fun. But sitting here now, older fathers of young kids, finally making a decent living and basking in the glitz at a Sunset Boulevard bistro, we asked ourselves, "Are we lucky, or what?"

"Absolutely! At our age, Mozart was dead."

" At Mozart's age, we were unemployed and chasing crazy women."

"We finally settled down. It's amazing isn't it. "

"No, *Don Giovanni's amazing.* This is pitiful!"

We laughed and sipped our seven-dollar ice teas. I looked up to see Jack Lemmon crossing the street to our café.

"Jack!" I yelled as if we were long lost friends.

I escorted him to the table, introduced him to Danny and

invited him to join us. He was on his way down the street to another lunch, but he chatted a moment and danced off. It was as if I'd planned this just to impress Danny.

"So, when does Marilyn Monroe stop by?"

"She's dead, Danny."

"Yes, but that would really impress me."

It was getting chilly in late November, but we kept the pool heated. Steam rose up from the water as we swam and ignored the fortune it must have been costing us. We had an Exiles' Thanksgiving Dinner with our houseguests and a bevy of New Yorkers who had moved to L.A. in search of work and sunshine.

The boys dressed for dinner, pants and shirts! And asked,

"Are we going to have turkey out here?"

"Of course!"

"Do they *have* turkey out here?"

" Yes, they fly them in. Or sometimes they fly in themselves."

"You mean, from Massachusetts?"

Danny jumped in. "Do you know what you'd be eating if you were having Thanksgiving in Turkey?"

"What?"

"Hot dogs!!"

What a relief. To know that other people's fathers made stupid jokes. And we pretended they were funny. I did point out to the boys that people in Los Angeles felt it was strange to celebrate Christmas where there was no snow, even though this was very much like the climate in Nazareth, where Christ lived.

"Yes, Dadoo, but not where Santa Claus lives!"

But, sitting around the big glass table, Navajo rugs hanging on the walls, the smell of ripe kumquats wafting in from the patio, I knew, as we sat amidst the comforting banter of old friends that this *was* temporary. The boys, in a way, had brought us out here, but I'd hope we would not stay long. We missed the changing of the leaves in fall. We missed snow. We missed walking to the corner for a slice of pizza. Hell, we just missed *walking*.

And we thought we should try to settle down somewhere where the boys could establish relationships with other kids. One afternoon, we invited the two boys who played Sam and Gabe over for a play date. To say it was odd to see the kids cast as Sam and Gabe on TV playing with the real Sam and Gabe at our house is an understatement. They played well together. Swimming, shooting water guns, etc. But that night in bed, as we asked them what stood out about the afternoon, Gabriel piped up.

"Peter doesn't know where Paris is."

Oh dear, my kids weren't going to become snobs were they? One trip to Europe and they were snobs?

"Neither of them knows what's the farthest planet from the sun."

Uh, oh. I didn't like the sound of this.

"Different things interest different people. Don't make value judgments."

"What's a value judgment?"

"When you … when you judge someone's worth … when you decide if you like someone or not by how much they know, or how they dress or what they eat or how they look."

"What's wrong with doing that?"

"A person can, for instance, know less than you but be a good person. A kind person. That should be more important."

"Can a person know a lot and *also* be a good person.?"

"Yes."

"Is it okay to like that kind of person?"

"Oh, yes."

"Great. We'll do that. Okay Gabe?"

" Okay."

" We'll do that, Dadoo."

"Okay."

But as the end of May approached and our lease was up, we changed our minds and decided to stay. It had been twenty plus years since my heyday in TV, and now, at last, having gotten a series on, I had some cachet. Minor cachet. Very, very minor cachet. But it beat none at all.

Julia is an athlete—a runner. And she was enamored of the warm weather and the ease of living and opted to stay also. The boys, bless 'em said, "Sure."

"Are we going to say in this big house?"

"No, no we can't afford this. But we'll find a very nice smaller place."

"And Dadoo, we won't have to worry about hurting the strange man's furniture."

"Right!"

"And Mommy says there's a good school right down the hill."

"Yes, Sammo, that's true."

"Gabe, we can *walk* to school."

"Samuel, Dadoo's going to take us in his beat up old convertible. Nobody walks out here."

Julia and I had stayed up nights agonizing over the decision of whether to stay or not, but something as gleeful as the idea that they could walk to school in a city where everybody drives excited the boys enough to make it an adventure.

"And maybe we can skate to school. It's all downhill."

"Yes, but Sam, coming home would be all uphill."

"So? Mommy's a jock. She could pull us."

Julia and I, "mature adults," had agonized. The kids just found a way to make it work.

SCENE: A SMALL RENTED HOUSE IN
STUDIO CITY, LOS ANGELES.

(The boys are playing ball with their parents in the small yard, as Pasquale, the 83-year-old Italian gardener whose services came with the rented house, calls Lee aside. He and the cherubic old gardener chat for a moment. Pasquale hands Lee a large manila envelope and Lee returns to the game.)

                    JULIA

Everything okay with the garden?

                    LEE

Fine.

                    SAMUEL

He's not going to put that smelly stuff on the lawn is he?

                    GABE

It's cow poop!

LEE

No, no, he's not.

JULIA

What did he give you?

LEE

Uh ... a screenplay.

GABE

Dadoo, he barely speaks English, how can he write a screenplay?

LEE

Honey, last week the pool guy, Vince, pitched me a TV series.

GABE

Is everybody in Hollywood a writer?

LEE

Just about.

SAM

I don't care what he is, as long as he doesn't put that smelly poop on the grass!

CHAPTER SEVEN

HITLER'S BATHROOM

We stayed out in L.A. another year, so I could try to sell a series. Of course, I was competing with my gardener and my pool guy.

We found a house on Sunshine Terrace.

It was much less expensive. Smaller. And cozier. In many ways we preferred this to the big house from year one. Also, when our friends asked us where we were living in L.A., we said blithely, "Sunshine Terrace—of course."

This house was unfurnished. Thank God, we didn't have to worry about breaking the crazy landlord's antiques. We rented furniture, and little by little we replaced the rental stuff with furniture Julia found on the street.

"Quick, get the car. There's a couch on Ventura Boulevard!"

The boys were happy. They started school. Kindergarten. They got real violins. One quarter sized. They were so small they looked like they came out of a cereal box. They began taking lessons. And they loved practicing. Real sounds came out. Not ones you particularly wanted to hear, but … It wasn't long before they learned to play "Twinkle, Twinkle." They could actually play a tune. And play it. And play it. And play it. To this day, when I hear "Twinkle" my teeth gnash.

An interesting pattern had developed with the boys. Twins are little bugs in petrie dishes. Because they grow up in the identical environment, you get your very own, pseudoscientific, in-house, child-study program. They each wanted alone time with us. And they'd figured out a one-up-early/one-to-bed late schedule to make it work. I don't think they sat down and planned it. It just ... kind of ... happened. And once they realized what it gave them, they set it in stone. Sam early. Gabe late. They got to *not* be twins.

It may not be true science, but it's fascinating. Sam would wake up early, when Julia got up to run. They'd hang out for awhile—cuddle and read. Then I'd get up and join them for breakfast. Gabe got up last and joined us. At night, Sam hit the sack first. I stayed up late to write and Gabe stayed up with me. While I sat at my desk, tapping away at the computer, Gabe sat beside me with a big yellow pad in hand scribbling away pretending to write. He couldn't write yet, but he wrote ... something. A word here or there. He filled the page. He was, as was his Dad at this moment, a writer. Every once in a while, I'd take the pad and read over his scribblings.

"What's this one about, Gabey?"

"It's about how I have to take care of Sam."

"You have to take care of Sam?"

"Oh yes. A lot. In the schoolyard, he runs around with his pacifier in his mouth. And I have to tell him, you can't have that in your mouth when we play kick ball. It's not safe. You could swallow it. And so I have to put it in my pocket until the game is over."

"Uh huh. What do the other kids think of Sam still using a pacifier at school?"

"Well, they think he's weird. But Sam rolls it around like a cigar and yells at them, 'Hey I like it. Bug off!'

"Bug off? Where did he learn to say that?"

"From you, Dadoo."

It was as sweet as sweet could be, those nights writing alone with Gabe. And Julia treasured her early mornings with Sam. On the other hand, Julia and I spent very little time alone with each other. We would have to put that on hold until they left for college.

One evening, after their bath, I was drying off Sam, Gabe having run naked and wet right into the den to plop himself in front of a National Geographic Special about elephants on TV. How do I remember that? Because he called me in later explain what was going on when there was shot of two elephants humping.

"Gabe, come back here you're still wet!"

"No I'm not, the couch dried me off!"

The boys didn't watch all that much TV. They'd seen plenty of Sesame Street when they were toddlers and loved *Thomas the Tank Engine,* and of course the annual *Charlie Brown's Christmas* and *The Grinch* and any Bugs Bunny episode. (Bugs was our hero—still is—because he was super confident and did not suffer fools gladly). But we liked to watch documentaries: The Life of Thomas Jefferson, or Thomas Edison, or the Wright Brothers. One of the documentaries we watched was about World War Two. One about Hitler. (There were so many shows about Hitler on the History Channel that it soon became known as the Hitler Channel). The boys knew very little if anything about Hitler. Oh they'd heard his name. His name comes up even without the help of documentaries. Because he's the epitome of evil, especially in a family that contains at least one Jew, his name comes up. Believe me. So they'd heard his name. And in this particular show, there was, in fact, some graphic footage of that evil. And we had to do some quick thinking about whether to snap off the TV when that footage appeared. We did. Which of course left us open to a barrage of questions about what they had missed. Why we had turned it off? And it left us having to explain the nature of the atrocities that we hadn't allowed them to see. That was really tough. But they saw enough of Mr. H's evils to know that he was bad. Very bad. He earned his evil epitome honestly.

In the bathroom, as I dried off Sam, he began goofing around. Jumping up and down and making airplane noises and pretending to ice skate in a puddle of water. I'm drying him and he's goofing around. He's getting out of hand. I finally hold him firmly and say, "Sam, you cannot goof around in the bathroom. You could get hurt. They say that the bathroom is the most dangerous room in the house." Sam looks at me, thinks a moment, and then asks soberly, "What's the most dangerous room in the world?" I looked at him. Thought. Shrugged. "I don't know Sam, what *is* the most dangerous room in the world?" He smiled, "Hitler's bathroom!!"

Well, I laughed. He laughed. And inside I thought, *Wow! How did he put that together?*

I didn't think of myself only as a comedy writer. I had an agent, years ago named Audrey Wood. She had been Tennessee Williams's agent. She was a legend. And I once confessed to her that I was reluctant to write comedy. She was a gruff woman. With a wonderful, large, gentle face. No nonsense. When you were talking to her on the phone, and the subject matter of the call was finished, she just hung up. No requisite small talk to end the conversation. Subject discussed—click! I thought, maybe someday I'll have the confidence to do that. Hasn't happened yet. But I was sitting in her office one day. It was twilight, just before Christmas, and she was particularly conversant on non-business subjects. Little things, like how she had to buy a particular kind of car because she was short and most cars wouldn't allow her to see over the steering wheel. So she ended up buying the new turtle shaped Rambler that everyone looked at as she drove by. Its futuristic design seemed so unlike her, she said, "I've been around a long time and I think people expect me to drive a little blue Buick. But this is the only car that lets me see out the windshield. I felt that was important!" We somehow got on to an idea for a play that I was working on. And I expressed my doubts about writing it, because it was a comedy. She leaned forward and patted my hand. "Yes, yes, Kalcheim, I know. You want to be a significant writer!"

From that moment on, I knew writing comedy would not make me a second class citizen.

And here I was in the midst of it—living in a house in Los Angeles, with a cozy home and a tiny pool and a view of the San Gabriel mountains—which naturally we called, "The Sam-Gabriel Mountains." I briefly also had a significant income. And all of this because of comedy. I had taught classes in writing television comedy, but I knew damn well comedy couldn't be taught. Oh, I could teach anyone how to write a sit-com. There was a formula. There were rules. If you followed the rules you could write something that we would *call* a sit-com. It might not be a *good* sit-com. But it could be called a sit-com. But I could not teach anyone to be funny. Am I saying, you have to be born funny? I don't know, but when the boys were two years old, maybe younger, just learning to talk, they were playing "train" in our laundry room up in our farmhouse in Massachusetts. (No farm, just house.) Both the boys were sitting on the floor with those striped overalls and caps and all sorts of paraphernalia that we thought looked like something that would be worn inside a train engine. Now sometime between birth and this moment, my wife and I had yelled out the expression "Alllll Aboard!" It was therefore general knowledge that this was what was yelled when a train was about to leave the station. Or we were about to leave the house. All Aboard! I peeked into the laundry room where train noises were rampant and asked how things were going. Gabe looked up at me and said that they were playing train. Then he pulled at a rope we'd tied between shelves of canned goods—the train whistle rope—and yelled, "All awood!" "What?" I said. "Allll awood." It took me all of ten seconds to get it. A board was a piece of wood. He was making a joke. "All awood" was a joke on "All aboard." Jesus, where did that come from? We didn't sit around the breakfast table deconstructing jokes. I certainly told my share of groaners. And my wife is very funny. But we didn't explain *how* you make a joke. And we rarely invented jokes. I did later on, when they became more sophisticated. Than what? All awood is pretty damned sophisticated.

Did each of my son's *learn* the construct of a joke from being around funny parents, or was there a comedy gene they inherited? My mother was funny. When I was a kid we lived next door to a Catholic family. We didn't interact much. I wasn't even sure how many members there were in their family. We heard voices come out of their open windows in the summer, but the only one I was sure who lived there was Danny. He was my age. And I don't think I said two words to him in the entire fifteen years I lived next door. But one day he and a few friends were playing in front of their house when I walked home from school, and they started shouting derisive remarks at me. Danny called me a matzo ball. When I told my mother she was incensed. She marched right over to our neighbors house and confronted Danny's mother and proclaimed, "Nobody calls my little matzo ball a matzo ball except me!"

My mother was a delightfully funny, witty women. She had a take that was as lethal as Jack Benny's when you said something off-putting. She could take an incident that had no comic value on the face of it and in the retelling make it hilarious. She recalled endlessly the time that a temp maid we had (middle class people had maids back in the fifties) had sipped a few too many drinks while making dinner. While my parents and their dinner guests were in the living room, the maid, trying strenuously to appear sober, swayed into the room, stood as still as she could and said to everyone, "Goodnight, I will see the remains of you in the morning."

At the time, I'm sure no one but my mother thought it funny, but when mom retold it, it landed. She even mimicked the woman's struggle to appear sober as she said, "the remains of you." So, I grew up listening to her filter jokes out of seemingly innocuous conversation. Why couldn't I have learned to be funny by listening to my mother? I learned how to put up storm windows from my father. A life lesson I thought I'd never ever have to use until I bought an eighteenth-century house that came with ancient storm windows (not eighteenth-century, but old) (Thanks, Dad!). I learned to look things up when I didn't know the answers to stuff. I can see my father at the dinner table, in the middle of a conversation about ... oh ... sheep herding in Ireland ... nodding to me and saying, "Get the Encyclopedia! Get the World Book!" But these were more conscious lessons. My mother never said, "This is what makes what I say funny." She had no idea. She just did it. Most people who talk or write funny claim they have no idea. How does a two year old kid, or a five year old kid, know how to construct a joke? Instantly. I didn't say to Sam, "Come up with a Hitler joke tomorrow by 6:00!" He did it on the spot. It had to be learned. Or at least absorbed.

That February, the boys dressed up for Presidents Day—one Lincoln, one Washington. That evening Sam decided to recite much of what he had learned of the Gettysburg Address. Still wearing his Lincoln outfit he began,

"Four score and seven years ago ..."

And went on as far as he could. We applauded. Then I got up.

"I'd like to recite the Gettysburg address."

"Do you know it, Dadoo?"

"Of course!"

Julia look at me doubtfully, "Really?"

"Of course. Know it cold."

I put Sam's Lincoln hat on my head and began.

"I would now like to recite Lincoln's Gettysburg address."

I took out a slip of paper and read, "135 Main Street, Gettysburg, Pennsylvania"

They laughed at the old joke. Booed. And threw pillows. But there it was. It was part of the fabric of the family.

But even great funnymen didn't necessarily have funny kids. Former comedy writer, now Senator, Al Franken said that his father was a working stiff, but loved comedy. Watched it all the time. Shared the love with his son. And I believe it was the sharing of it, the fun of laughing together that motivated the son to want to be funny.

Comedy can't be taught, but it can be learned. The same way we learn diligence, responsibility, even generosity, we learn to be funny. So what I learned from my kids' precocious comedic flare has nothing to do with comedy. It has to do with realizing *how* your kids learn from you.

Those of you with teenagers know that you cannot tell them anything. They already know it. This is a cliché, but it's true often enough for you to avoid even trying to tell them something. But the good news is, you don't have to tell them *anything.* They already know it. They learned it from you! Even though you don't remember telling them what it is you wanted to tell them. They learned it from you, by example. If you work hard, your kids will be inspired by it. If you make jokes or listen to music or sing in the shower—if you express joy, your children will learn to express joy. You can't say to a child "Express more joy Richard." It doesn't work. And it really sounds lame.

There are things that cannot be taught—either because they're too complicated to teach or they will fall on unwilling ears if you try to teach them. Not to worry. For every four-letter word your kids pick up from you, they will pick up a great many more important things. Enjoy life, work hard, and be kind to your mother, and your kids will, if you haven't bought them an expensive computer game that takes them away from your world, embrace your world. And then surprise you when they reveal they have learned a lesson you've never taught.

All of this, they taught me.

SCENE: THE DEN OF A HOME IN
STUDIO CITY, CALIFORNIA.

(A baseball game is on the television. Lee sits with Samuel and Gabriel watching.)

LEE

Okay, runner on first, nobody out, the count's 3 and 1 on the batter. It's a good count for a hit and run.

SAM

Don't you always want to hit?

GABE

And run?

SAM

And run?

LEE

No. On a hit and run count, like 3 and 1, when the pitcher *has* to throw a strike, the runner can take off on the pitch, because there is a good chance the batter will hit it. If it's a hit the runner will get to third, if it's a grounder he can avoid the double play. It's aggressive baseball.

GABE

What happens if the ball is hit right to the first baseman?

SAM.

In the air. Bam!

GABE

Bam!

LEE

The ... uh ... the runner is *screwed*.

GABE

Is that a baseball term?

CHAPTER EIGHT

DAMNED YANKEES?

Baseball is the game writers like to write about. I don't mean baseball writers. Novelists. There is something about the game. It's not really a team sport. It's sport about grace and timing and individual skill. It's a chess match in a field. It has no clock. It has an infinite number of dramatic situations, depending on the number of men on base, the number of outs, the kind of pitcher, the speed of the runners, even the position of the sun in the afternoon sky (when they play a rare day game). Despite the love of the long ball, it's game of tactics that rewards the small things. The bunt, the steal, the sacrifice. What other sport has a play called a sacrifice? No wonder writers love it. (I am, in fact, listening to a ball game as I write this.)

We stayed another year in L.A., as I hoped, with a "smile and a shoeshine" to generate some work. Julia was sewing seeds for her future as a literary agent by sitting in with a group of writers each week as they read and criticized their work. The boys were now in first grade, chaffing at the restrictions of having to wait quietly in line before filing into school and sitting quietly in class until called upon. The free exchange of ideas at home at our ragtag undisciplined dinner table discussions did *not* prepare them for the etiquette at school. It was our third year there, and we were integrating ourselves into a familiar American suburban lifestyle: lessons upon lessons—violin, piano, tap, (Tap? They adored *Singing in the Rain*.) and, of course, soccer and baseball.

I loved baseball when I was kid. And it isn't easy to love something when you're not good at it. My hand-eye coordination stinks. In the army I was a "bollo" on the shooting range. I could not hit the target. I figured out a way of raising my score. I counted the number of seconds when the pop up target would fall by itself, so I learned to fire just before it fell and get credit for knocking it over. If I were to go into a real battle, I would have needed a few shills in the enemy line to fall down every five seconds, and then the others would be so intimidated by my shooting skills that surrender would be imminent. Fortunately I never got into a real battle. Fortunately for me and the United States Army. As a baseball player, my hand-eye coordination problem was compounded by the fact that I was afraid of the ball. As a ball came whistling at me, all I could think was, "This ball could kill me. Or if not, it could hit me in the head and knock me out and make me stupid or comatose or incapacitated for life. I'm going to be a writer. (Yes, I knew that at twelve years old. I wrote a screenplay at twelve about a platoon of soldiers in World War II based on all my harrowing wartime experience.) A writer was not going to be much of a writer if he was comatose. A fly ball is hit. I look up. I see it. But I can't judge where it is. I run to get under it. Or as under it as I think I am, which is not really under it, and then as it descends I start thinking, of course, this ball could hit me in the head. And you know the rest. But for some damned reason, I loved the game. I never fantasized about winning the academy award for my World War II film. I fantasized about driving in the winning run in a major league ball game. And marrying Esther Williams. But that's another story.

You wonder as your children grow up whether they will

acquire things like your hit-me-on-the-head-fly-ball phobia, or whether they, like their father, will learn to love baseball more as a concept than a game. Or, would they, like their mother, who rock climbed up sheer cliffs as a teenager (she once climbed up a stone fireplace in a restaurant on a bet), be fearless.

You look for clues. Early soccer games, they'd bunch up around the ball like the other six year olds, leaving no one free to pass the ball to. Good, I suppose. They want to be part of the action. But you watch to see, when a player charges at them or a kid kicks the ball at them, if they shy away, if they are fearless or cautious. But does it matter, if they're having fun? The last thing you want to do is overcompensate for your fears and say something stupid like, "Charge into him—the ball can't hurt that much."

I think because of their being twins, they didn't need a father or mother coach. They coached each other. And it was a great lesson in laid-back fathering to realize that instruction coming from their peers—their brother, their friend—is easier to take. Even if it's cruel as it can sometimes be. Then that puts you in the enviable position of comforting your child, of being above the fray.

"What he meant when said, 'Don't be a ball hog, jerk,' is ..."

"I know what he meant, Dadoo."

"He just wants you to pass more."

"That doesn't make me a jerk. He's a jerk for calling me a jerk!"

"Yes, I think you're right."

They even begin to understand the strengths and limits of their talents without you having to say a thing. They both played T-ball. Sam was good at it. Gabe less so. So when Samuel graduated to "coach-pitch" Gabe chose to go to art classes at the museum. But he wanted to watch all of Sam's games. When Sam hit a game-winning home run, Gabe jumped up and down for joy and rushed to embrace his brother. I was moved, not so much at Sam's game winning hit, but at Gabe's joyful, generous reaction.

Would that Gabe had been my father when I was a young camper, upset at my inability to catch a fly ball. He would have said, as he does say today, "But look at what you *do*, do well."

He actually said to me when I was down in the dumps at the awful vicissitudes of my business, "But Dadoo, look at all the plays of yours that have been produced. You just keep working. You're amazing."

Kids find a path for themselves, sometimes through great disappointment, and especially if their parents are imperfect, they respond and then give back.

"You're amazing."

It was October, 1996 in Los Angeles. Back in Massachusetts the leaves would have been changing. The Berkshire Hills would be awash in oranges and yellows and reds. Twenty years back, when Bonnie Franklin and I were dating, she used to tease me because I would never visit her in Los Angeles in October.

"Of course not. Not when your precious leaves are changing!"

And she would laugh delightfully. And October is also World Series time, and in '96, the Yankees were in the World Series. The games came on at five in the afternoon on the west coast, so we could watch some games and the boys could make their bedtime. Growing up in Philadelphia, I had hated the Yankees. The Yankees always won. Boring. The Phillies always lost. Hopeless, but not boring. Well, not completely hopeless. They could just maybe someday win it all. That gave me hope. Well, when you're a kid you always have hope.

And my hope was vindicated when my Phillies team finally won the pennant in 1950—and then dashed when were beaten by the Yankees in the World Series, four zip! Damned Yankees! Humiliating. Could it be true? Some teams were just better? I discovered later, when I became a Yankee convert, it is possible to root for a team that is so good you expect them to win. You have confidence they will win. (They are the best.) And that uneasy feeling I always had with the Phillies—the feeling that with the go-ahead runs on base, the hitter would *not* drive them in, just wasn't there. Bad teams manage *not* to get hits with runners on. If there is a metaphor for failure in life it surely must be not getting a hit with a runner in scoring position. And so what happens is that every time runners do get into scoring position, as the batter stands in, you get that sickening feeling that ... it's over. Don't get excited. It's over. And after a while you give up. You're disgusted. And start drinking. And you lose your job. And your wife leaves you. And you walk into the ocean, like James Mason in *A Star is Born*.

I didn't feel that way rooting for those magical late '90s Yankees. They did everything right. They played little ball, big ball, any damned kind of ball that won ball games. Watching those games, I knew the exquisite feeling of complete confidence. There was no tension. My guys were the best. They would do it. Ah! And having come late to rooting for a good team was not that dissimilar to having come later to fatherhood. I could not have adored being father more, because I *finally* got it right. My obsession with the Yanks—and my obsession with my family— were all part of this great late appreciation for life. For, at long last, getting it right.

On this October day in 1996, I was still a residual Yankee hater. But the Yanks had regrouped. This was a new team. And they were in the series against Atlanta. And I could teach the boys to the nuances of the game by watching it on TV while they asked questions.

"Why is a batter out if he bunts with two strikes?"

"Uh, well, I think ... back in the old days of baseball, the 1890's, batters would foul off pitches just get the pitcher really tired. And one pitcher, for the Cincinnati Reds threw seventy six pitches, all of them fouled off by a Chicago Cubs batter. So, they made the rule; two strikes, you bunt foul—you're out."

"Dadoo, you made that up."
"Yes, I did."
"But, it sounds good."
"Thanks."
"So, do you know why?"
"Haven't a clue!"

We watched as the Yankees came back from a two-nothing deficit, having lost both games at Yankee Stadium. They won four straight and won the series 4–2. I taught the boys all the nuances of the game. Go Nuance!

"Why can a runner run to first if the catcher drops a third strike?"

"Ah, well … that's because there was a catcher for the Red Sox named 'Thumbs Strickland' who was a terrific hitter, and the Yankees tried to keep him out of the lineup as much as possible, so they forced the league to adopt the 'dropping the third strike' rule—which 'Thumbs' did a lot and allowed the Yanks to get more men on base and beat the Red Sox."

"I don't believe that."

"Okay, do you believe that the Red Sox sold Babe Ruth to the Yankees because the Sox owner needed the money to invest in a Broadway musical, *No, No Nanette*?"

"No!"

Well, Gabey, that's true."

"But there is no 'Thumbs' Strickland."

"Nope."

"Was there a *No No Nanette*?"

"You bet Sammo. Wanna hear some of the songs?"

"Not during the game!"

As we watched the Yankee game, something happened. These were not only new Yankees, these were different Yankees. A different kind of team. Not the power teams of Mantle and Maris. They played little ball. Hit and run. Steal. Bunt. Great pitching.

And graceful fielding. Just watching Bernie Williams run defined grace. But most of all, most of all, there was Derek Jeter. He was a rookie. He was handsome. And he was good. He was good in the way that filled your chest. He made things happen. When he came up with men on you knew, you just damn well knew that he would do anything to drive in that run. He was able to take an inside pitch and twist his body and hit it to right field. He could get on first. Steal second. Go to third on a grounder and score on a fly ball. Do that three times a game and win the game on his own. He was a cheerleader, always standing on the top step of the dugout, encouraging his teammates . And he was a leader. And his being handsome in that modern, cross culture way (His father is black, his mother Asian) made him a symbol of what is best about America. He was the melting pot. He was good. And he was a synthesis of all the good things we could be. And, maybe most of all for an old Yankee hater, he was the leader of a different team. An unboring team. A team that won, but won in a different way each time. A smart team. I fell in love with them.

And the boys fell in love with them. And baseball. What began as a lesson in the nuances of the game on a second-hand couch in Studio City evolved into as important and cozy a family ritual as reading stories to them at bedtime. Story reading was not just a one-way proposition; we read, they listen. Your kids ask questions about the stories, and you respond and comment. They get caught up in the narrative from the simplest silly adventures of *Winnie the Pooh* to the dark and complex wanderings of *Huckleberry Finn*. Watching baseball with the boys was, in its way, as cozy and intimate as snuggling with them in bed. Talk, strategy was being exchanged on that couch, but love of the game was being felt. And love of those players who played so well. And love of each other was manifest in every move and in every word and especially in the exuberant gesture that became a ritual, with all of us standing up on the couch and cheering at the top of our lungs when the Yankees came from behind and rallied to win!

I can still feel the joy now, remembering, standing on one couch or another, a son on each side, jumping up and down, sagging into the pillows and screaming as Julia runs into the room knowing something good has occurred, and smiling at the sight of her men celebrating, she joins us in a pile to watch the glorious replay.

My love of baseball and my love of family intertwined into a magical pursuit that would last throughout their childhood. Watching those games I became myself at their age, listening to games with my Dad. And when, as a parent, you become yourself as a child, and recreate that same comforting pleasure, your world reduces itself to the simplest, most basic experience. Parent and child are inseparable. Who is who? You are both. There is no finer bliss.

SCENE: A BUS AS IT PASSES THE COLISEUM IN ROME, ITALY.

(Samuel and Gabriel, seven years old, point to it with excitement.)

GABE

Mommy, Dadoo, look, that's the coliseum.

LEE , JULIA

Yes!

GABE

In person.

LEE, JULIA

Yes!

SAM

Do they still use it?

JULIA

Oh, for concerts and things.

(Gabe turns to Sam, and speaking with great authority)

GABE

That's where the Gladiators fought.

SAM

I know, Gabe.

GABE

And where they fed the Christians to the Lions!

SAM

Yeah, but we're half *Jewish,* so the Lions would only eat half of us!

CHAPTER NINE

ROMAN (WORKING) HOLIDAY

After having lived in New York and Massachusetts and three years in Los Angeles, in the fall of the boys seventh year we were fortunate to have another choice: Rome.

My old alma mater, Trinity College, Hartford had a study abroad program there. I had become friendly with the college's new president, Evan Dobelle. Evan was doing terrific things at this rather staid old school—specifically an initiative to help vitalize the crumbling community around the college. He felt the school had a obligation to its neighbors. It should not be an ivory tower, but an economic and cultural engine in the community. He pulled it off. In the midst of his reformative zeal, we met at my college reunion and later that summer had a picnic lunch with our families, where he turned to me and casually said, "How'd you like to teach in Rome?"

Julia almost fell off the picnic bench.

"Yes! When? We'll pack tonight."

Evan had seen a play of mine at the Williamstown Theatre

Festival and knew that I had taught playwriting at N.Y.U. He didn't know that Julia spoke pretty good Italian or that I wanted to move as far away from Hollywood as possible.

It would mean a new home and a new school for the boys. What did they think?

"Dadoo, is your Italian as bad as your French?"

"I don't know any Italian. I'll have to learn it over there. I'll take classes with the students."

"You can teach classes and take them at the same time?"

"Is that legal?"

"I think so. In Italy."

"What about us? We don't speak Italian."

"You can learn. It'll be fun."

"Mommy," Sam blurted out, "say something in Italian."

"Voglio andare a Roma."

"What's that mean?"

"I wish to go to Rome."

"Voglio ... "

"Andare ... "

"Andare ... "

"A Roma."

"A Roma. Voglio andare a Roma."

"Good Sam."

"I'm ready. Gabe?"

"Voglio andare a Roma.

And we went.

Trinity College is located in a section of Rome called "The Aventino"—a lovely, mostly residential, neighborhood that runs along both sides of the Via Aventino, a broad street that is anchored on one end by a large pyramid (Il Pyramide) and the other by the old chariot raceway—The Circus Maximus. The college resides in an old convent at the top of a hill over the Aventino, and still shares its facilities with the Convent nuns.

It's a very simple setting—a few classrooms, a small auditorium, and a dormitory, nestled around a quiet cloister that abuts the convent garden. The antithesis of Hollywood.

We lived in an apartment provided by the college, a short walk from the campus. The apartment was a roomy first floor flat, with two bedrooms, a living room, a small kitchen, and furniture that looked like it had been bought at an estate sale from a down-at-the-heels Italian count. It was clunky, but comfortable. The apartment was dark. The mattresses on the bed were punishing. But we were in Rome! We were in heaven!

The boys had completed first grade in Los Angeles and would start second in Rome. We had schooled them before the trip on some Roman history—illustrated—and pop-up books that told them the history of the thousand year empire. That summer, before we left, they were so excited they were dressing up as Roman soldiers. From old curtain material, Julia fashioned tunics and capes, and they wore sandals and carried swords (cardboard ones fashioned by Julia) and shields (pot lids). They already knew about Caesar, his reign and demise, and Augustus, who expanded the empire to its farthest reaches. The idea that we were actually going to live in the city where these men lived was unimaginably exciting. It's one thing to see a pop-up of the Coliseum; it's another to actually walk into it.

The delight of traveling with kids this young is that changing schools is no big deal. There is nothing crucial that they're learning in the early grades, and things like basic math and reading skills begin at home. But twins have an enormous advantage in moving from school to school. They have each other. Some of our friends told us, "We can't do what you did. Our daughter doesn't want to leave her friends." Sam and Gabe had each other—a constant best friend.

Thanks to the largess of their grandmother, we sent them to an International School, where English was the "lingua franca."

A bit of a mistake. Had we just tossed them into an Italian public school they would have struggled and probably survived, but we thought it'd be difficult enough adjusting to a new home. A new language seemed a bit much. We thought they'd learn Italian there in the schoolyard. They did. "Che schivo!" Which means basically, "How gross." But they didn't learn to speak much Italian. The school drew kids from all over the world, children of diplomats and U.N. workers. As it turns out, what Italian they did learn, they pronounced impeccably. I, on the other hand, took the beginner's Italian class at the college, learning enough to shop and make my way around. But I mangled pronunciations. I had the hand gestures down, but that's about it. My previous French experience caused me to speak Italian with a French accent. So I would say, "bonjour-no" instead of "buon giorno." I didn't realize it until the man at the newsstand, from whom I bought my daily *International Herald Tribune,* starting addressing me in French. He thought I was French! Well, what the hell, at least he thought I was European!

The apartment was situated at the top of a hill above the Baths of Caracalla and one half block off the square in front of the Church of St. Salbo. The Square was backed by a small leafy park and dotted by a half dozen little stores. In the morning an open air market burst to life there, and all of the locals rushed there to shop and gossip. A ritual soon developed. We'd rise in time to give the boys some breakfast, American cereal that tasted better than the same brand made in America. (They were right. Special K is better in Italy than in America). And the pre-made toast, smeared with Nutella. Mmmmmmmmmm. We took them to the corner to await the school bus. We'd visited the school several days before and the boys felt comfortable riding the bus there with their new schoolmates. The first day, a huge tourist-like bus pulled up. They got on. We were impressed. Fancy schmancy. It drove off to pick up the bulk of the kids in front of the FAO building (U.N. Food Assistance Organization). But, the next day the bus route had been reconfigured and so they sent a smaller bus, half the size, to pick up the boys. By the end of the week, the school had again reorganized its bus pickups and a bus that looked like a half-sized minivan appeared and whisked the boys away. By Monday, I told the boys to expect a guy on a motorcycle to drive up and say "hop on." God forbid you should miss the bus. Which happened frequently enough because ... after all ... these were Italians, and Mussolini was long gone, and so the buses didn't always run on schedule. And neither did we. Their school was in an un-findable neighborhood. The first time we missed the bus, we just hailed a taxi and took them there. Unlike the French taxi driver he was not dismissive of our struggles with his language. He was friendly and charming. But he couldn't find the place! But with our help and a good map, he did. We decided we'd tough it out and go home by bus. Two and a half hours later we were home. Henceforth, we always erred on the safe side and got out to the corner extra early, so as not to miss the bus. Whatever size it came in.

After the bus picked up the boys, I went for my *Herald Tribune* and Julia went back to the apartment to check her e-mail. (e-mail was new then, and you were not likely to get much ... much less any spam.) She'd do the laundry, which was interesting, since there was no dryer and very little room to hang it outside to dry. During the rainy season we hung everything inside, and the moisture evaporating from our sheets hung all over the place, causing a fog to rise inside the apartment. I'd do the shopping. And on the weekends, when the boys were home, we could all go together. Samuel and Gabriel were seeing a world outside the supermarket. We had come from L.A., where they had seen airplane hangar-sized markets that had everything from linguine to lawn mowers. And now they were introduced to the little town square where the butcher and the baker and the fruit lady all had their own little stalls. Our refrigerator was so small, you couldn't really shop for more than a day's worth of food, so I had to go every day. And I loved it.

The grocers in the stalls soon got to know me and know the boys. Sam and Gabe began to understand the difference between shopping and buying. The difference between wheeling a huge cart down the aisles of a fluorescent-lighted supermarket and just pulling items off the shelves and walking from stall to stall, checking out whether Fabrizio's peppers looked better than Isabella's. Debating the issue. Taking Isabella's advice that today was good day for peaches and not for grapes. Even making mistakes when asking Georgio the butcher for chicken breasts; we requested "filleta de pollo" which turned out to be thin slices. And then realizing at home that we could bread them and fry them quickly in olive oil and lemon and have something more delicious than we had planned. Shopping was surprises. What looked good that day. You didn't carry a list. You saw what looked good or what Georgio said was good, and you went for it. Shopping wasn't something you had to do in your busy day. It was an event. It was a social event. You looked forward to it. And if you were feeling particularly good after you shopped, you stopped at the corner bar and had a cornetti (an Italian croissant) and a cup of espresso. The boys began to understand the delicious pursuit of every day life. There was no such thing as fast food in Italy. *Eating* was an event. Buying the food, cooking the food, or going to a *ristorante* for food was not to be hurried. I remember, after moving back to New York, we were sitting in restaurant, and I stole a look at my watch, and Gabriel said, "Dadoo, where do we have to go? We're here."

One day we ventured to the big market in Testaccio, the rambling, blue-collar neighborhood nearby on the Via Marmoratta. (The marble street, the street where, in Roman times, the marble was unloaded on the docks after it had come by sea and down the Tiber all the way from the marble quarries in Carrara) This market was twenty times the size of the one in St. Salbo. They had everything from fresh squid to plastic sandals. I wanted to roast a chicken and stuff it with Italian herbs. But I didn't know the butcher there. I just found a chicken I liked.

"Isn't it kind of... yellow, Dadoo?"

"Yes. Well ... it's ... I think ... .Italian chickens are yellow."

"Shouldn't you ask?"

I wasn't sure how to ask why his chicken was yellow. I told the boys it was fine. Bought it. Took it home. Roasted it. It was so tough we almost broke our teeth on it. A rubber chicken. I later found out from a friend.

"Oh the yellow ones are for boiling! You have to boil them all day before you can eat them."

I was out of my league in the big market on the Via Marmoratta.

But there was an excitement of being out of your league. Of having to work hard just to communicate the most basic things. We'd stop once a week at the little mom and pop store at the corner of the square to buy milk and cheese and Special K. Samuel asked me as we walked in the first time, "Dadoo, if you don't speak Italian, how are you going to buy Special K for us?"

"Watch!"

I strutted in like a confident New Yorker abroad.

"Peor favore. Voglio Special K."

The old man behind the counter, the "Pop" of "Mom and Pop" blinked. Knitted his brows.

"Special K?"

"Cereal-e" I pronounced cereal as if it were an Italian word. I was actually pretty close, but not close enough for pop. He shrugged. I walked over and pointed to the cereal display behind the counter and pointed to the top. "Special K."

Pop got his grabber pole and moved to the cereals. And when he stopped at the Special K I shouted. "Si! Si! Grazie" And he pulled down a box. Gabe turned to me.

"But Dadoo, if you're going to point, you don't have to speak any Italian."

"But, Gabey I'm establishing a relationship with the shop owner. If I come in once a week and ask for "Special K," then I won't have to point."

"If you come in once a week, they're gonna *know* what you want when you walk in the door."

SCENE: A TRATTORIA IN FLORENCE, ITALY. LEE, JULIA, SAM, AND GABE ARE HAVING LUNCH AFTER A MORNING OF VISITING CHURCHES AND SEEING FRESCOES.

SAM

Dadoo, do people paint frescoes anymore?

LEE

Sure, but they call them murals.

SAM

Where are they? The new ones?

JULIA

There's a big one at Lincoln Center. Painted by Marc Chagall.

SAM

How come all the ones in Italy are of saints and stuff?

LEE

That's because they were painted inside the churches and they were paid for, commissioned, by very rich, very religious families.

SAM

If I become rich, I'm going to commission a fresco!

JULIA

Of what?

SAM

Of ... Bugs Bunny!

CHAPTER TEN

THE BLUE GROTTO

One of the perks of the Trinity program was that, as a faculty member, I got to go on the class trips. All of us went. Julia and the boys and I traveled with the students on their trips to Florence and Venice and Naples. I can say without reservation that Samuel and Gabriel learned more, while they were having more fun, on those trips than any other adventure in their lives. The trips were led by the director of the program, Livio Pestilli—the definition of a gentleman and a scholar—a sweet, smart, soft-spoken man who had moved with his parents, to Rochester N.Y., as a teenager, married his high school sweetheart and after graduate work in the states, moved back to Italy to teach. It was his sagacity and flexibility that allowed me to teach playwriting in a program principally geared for Italian art and history. But he understood that if I urged the students to write about their experiences in Rome it would make them that much richer. And I loved teaching students with little writing experience. They were sponges. Ready to learn. Full of enthusiasm for learning something new. And there was a fabulous contagion being on the trips with them. I'll never forget a couple of the students, carrying our boys on their shoulders through the narrow medieval streets of Florence, as the boys waved to everyone, as if they were Renaissance dukes greeting their patrons.

On that trip to Florence, after the train ride up from Rome, we were all led to the Uffizi palace to see, outside, the Michelangelo statue of David and, inside, the vast collection of Italian art: from Giotto and Bellini, to Veronese and Botticelli. We were there over four hours, and not once did the boys say, "Can we go now?" They followed Livio's careful, insightful comments with infinite patience as we toured the museum. Julia and I were impressed. Of course, the next day, when Livio led us in and out of Florentine churches to see frescoes, Sam, exhausted at seeing so many frescoes, suddenly piped up, doing an imitation of Livio as we passed another church, "Oh, we *must* go in here. The frescoes in here are the best. Better than the best. *Magnifico!*"

The last night in Florence, we went to a concert of Vivaldi's "The Four Seasons," and the boys, the budding violinists, sat next to each other to better comment on the players. In the midst of the concert, Gabe leaned to Sam and whispered something about the recital. From behind us we heard a loud "clap." What was that? Someone swatting a mosquito? The concert continued. Sam leaned to Sam and *whispered* again. "Clap!" I turned and saw a stocky, tight-faced woman glaring at us. When the piece was finished, the woman rose and confronted Julia and me and in a brusque German accent, announced, "Kinder should not be allowed to attend zese concerts!"

I smiled, and nodded and said to her, "If the kinder are not allowed to attend these concerts, pretty soon interest in music will die off, and there will be *nobody* at these concerts!"

The fraulein had pigeon-holed our "kinder" as being too restless and disinterested to appreciate the music. They must be whispering to each other about how bored they were. *Julia and I* were the ones struggling to stay awake. The boys were juiced by the music.

The same persistence and patience prevailed when we traveled to Naples to see Pompeii on a stifling hot day. It's a long ride from Rome to Naples, and Livio took the microphone in the front of the bus to point out sites along the way, "Look to your left, up on that hilltop is the castle of Monte Casino, where one of the deadliest battles of World War II took place, as the American troops fought the encamped Nazis there to clear the road to Rome." The students were getting restless. The trip was long, and they were tired. Suddenly, I saw Sam and Gabe whispering to Livio, and the next thing we knew they were holding the microphone as Sam announced, "We'd like to do a few songs. These are songs you probably don't know. We learned them from our folks' old records." And, Sam sang out, "Ya gotta accentuate the positive / Eeeliminate the negative / Latch on the affirmative /Don't mess with Mister In Between!" The students woke up and laughed and cheered. Gabe took the mike, and both of them sang, "Another bride/ Another Groom/ Another Sunny/ Honeymoon/ Another season/ Another reason/ For makin' whoopee."

Livio laughed. There's Italian renaissance history. And American pop song history. And the two were fusing nicely on the road to Naples.

As we toured the ghost city of Pompeii, the heat so oppressive we put up umbrellas to shade ourselves, Livio pressed on through the ruins, and again the boys were wide-eyed at the sight of a culture frozen in time—at the sight of a young boy, their age, petrified in stone, curled in fetal position on his bed, as the ash from Vesuvias engulfed him two thousand years ago.

Then down to the wharf and onto the hydrofoil and off to Capri.

Capri, as you probably know, is a huge tourist stop. A small island rising out of the Mediterranean just off the picturesque Amalfi coast, it teems with visitors—day visitors from Southern Italy and overnighters from Germany, Japan, and the U.S., crowding the narrow streets and curio shops. We encamped, fortunately at the top of the island in Anacapri—away from the crowds and high enough to see three hundred and sixty degrees to the ocean on all sides. On our first full day, Livio led us all on a walk across the top of the island, winding along roads that edged along steep cliffs down to the sea on our way to Emperor Tiberius's villa. Arriving at the well preserved remains of the emperor's home-away-from-Rome, Livio pointed out that Tiberius lived here in luxury during most of his reign, away from the unrest in Rome, the intrigues against his rule, and the rebellion in the Roman colony in Jerusalem, where an iconoclastic young Jew, named Joshua was arrested, tried, convicted, and crucified. While Tiberius partied on.

On the way back on the path from the villa, we stopped at a restaurant perched on the side of the cliff overlooking the natural arches that stood below in the sea. Fig trees shaded us as we ate and luxuriated in plates of prosciutto and fresh picked figs while we gazed out at the view. Gabe looked at me with his intense brown eyes, his auburn hair blowing in the sea breeze.

"Dadoo, this really is incredible."

"What sweetie? The food? The view? The trip?

"Everything."

The first time I traveled out of the country was not until the summer after I had graduated college. I was twenty-two. My father had taken his first trip abroad with my mom when he was fifty-one years old. My sons were seven. There are those who say such adventures are wasted on children this age. I felt lucky at twenty two, and my father, the same at fifty one to see the world outside of home. The boys had been traveling abroad since they were four. And knew very well how lucky they were. And how every moment, from seeing an Emperor's villa to eating a fresh fig overlooking the sea was precious. And not to be forgotten.

The day before we left Capri we bussed down to the shore

adjacent the famous blue grotto. It is a cave whose mouth opens to the sea. Tourists row boats inside to see the cave. Livio's assistant, Francesco, told us to go late in the day, when there were no tourists or boats, and to swim in. But when we arrived, it was high tide. When the small waves would break on the shore, the mouth of the grotto would be completely covered in water. We'd have to swim out to the mouth, and when there was as opening between the waves, we'd have to swim into the cave. This scared Sam, and he decided to wait on shore with some of the students who'd accompanied us. Surprisingly, Gabe wanted to go. He'd heard what a wondrous site it was inside. So he willed himself to do it. He also knew that his mother, though fearless, was careful. Julia, Gabe, and I swam out from shore and toward the cave's mouth. Gabe climbed on Julia's back, and together we swam to the cave's mouth, waited for the water to recede, the mouth to open, and then we all shouted, "Go!" and quickly swam through the mouth and into the cave! And wondrous it was. The light bouncing on the water from outside reflected up and into the dark cave and glowed! We treaded water in this dark, dark cave while around us the water glowed an incandescent blue-green. Gabe, clinging to his mother's back, had pushed himself to do something that had scared him, and now seeing the reward for his daring, the phenomena of the glowing water, he hugged his mother from behind.

"Mommy, it's beautiful. It was worth it."

After that moment, if ever I hesitate to try something that scares me, even just a bit, I see Gabe in the blue grotto, filled with wonder, and I forge ahead.

CHAPTER ELEVEN

SKETCHES

Whenever I travel, I take my sketchbook, my watercolors, and my drawing pen. As we wander around cities filled with architectural surprises, I can stop and paint. My family tolerantly stops with me or walks slowly ahead as I sketch. *Or* the boys take leaves from my pad, extra brushes, and pens and go at it themselves. And often, they have their own

sketch pads which double for playing tic tac toe or hangman while on a long train ride. We tend to cram a lot into our days. Seeing as much as we can, and sketching not only slows us down, but encourages us to really *see* what we're seeing, whether it's the twin sixteenth-century churches at the south end of the Piazza di Popolo in Rome or a row of Hausman-era houses in Paris, with their rounded mansard roofs and huge shuttered windows.

We would sit in the Piazza, on the fountain, dipping our brushes in the water, looking at the churches, painting, drawing, dipping, listening to the water swooshing out of the fountain, and smelling the pastry and coffee from a nearby café. Sometimes,

after a frantic sightseeing morning, I'd go off by myself to sketch alone. Or Julia would take an afternoon run, and I'd take the boys back to a favorite spot we'd missed earlier, and now that we had time, we'd do our little paintings. One afternoon in Paris, while we sat picnicking in the Place De Voges, we made drawings of the houses on the lovely brick square where Victor Hugo lived and wrote *Les Miserables*.

Sitting in front of the Pantheon in Rome, sketching it, chatting about how oddly this Roman building sits in this Renaissance square, makes just the looking at it an experience. As you sketch, you marvel at its dome, because you realize how hard it is to get the shape of the dome, just right.

"It doesn't have to be perfect. Just give a wash of color where the dome is and draw half the dome. It's just an impression."

"Like this?"

"Yes. And you don't have to draw every column completely. Three or four and just a dark stroke of, light brown or gray, and then a line or two to indicate the rest. See?"

"Neat."

Looking through the sketchbook when you get home reminds you not only of the thing itself, but of the time you spent sketching it. Drawing it cements it in your mind and recycles the experience of that drawing over and over again.

Our last trip was to Venice. In November. It can be quite chilly. And we were advised to take boots for the boys, because it was the time of year of the "aqua alta"—the exceptionally high tides that flood many of the streets and squares. This magical city was, because of the weather, devoid of tourists, and it had a somewhat spooky feeling about it. The glorious piazzas, the usually heavily trafficked canals, were empty. Venice in the last decade or so had lost much of its permanent population. Modern Italians found it just too confining to live there.

The younger generation wanted to be able to drive their fast cars and *motorinos* down the streets of Rome and Milan and crush together on weekend nights at the grand Piazza Narvona in Rome, or even the smallest town square in Puglia, and smoke and drink and party. Venice was almost too intimidating for that kind of thing. Oh, there were kids. And there were parties, but the old

palazzos on the grand canal were the part-time homes of wealthy American and European retirees. The once crowded little apartments in the winding back alleys had seen their occupants off to kitchen staffs in Trieste or the auto plants in Turin. This magnificent city had become a museum. A living museum. The water was high. St Marks square was flooded, and to get around it or across you had had to walk on wooden boardwalks that had been erected. Julia and I had to use them—we didn't have boots. But we'd gotten the boys shiny yellow ones, and they gleefully walked in the shin-high water, splashing along with many of the other students. The idea that people actually lived in a city where there were no cars and that the taxis were water taxis blew them away.

"Here comes our bus. Here comes the *vaporetta!*"

"Get on the front, so we can see everything."

"And get wet from the spray."

After a long day of museums and churches under Livio's guidance, we wandered over to the Piazza St. Marco to have an evening cappuchino. The tide had ebbed, and we could sit at a café without getting our feet wet. The boys zipped up their "up" coats as opposed to their down coats against the evening chill. The warm coffee felt good. A violinist came by serenading.

"Here, Gabey, give him a few lire."

"He's not that good."

"He's an old man working hard. Give him this."

Gabey gave him the lire and thanked him.

"Grazie."

Sam stuck out his hand. "He's working really hard. Can I give him some too?"

And he did. And we sat back and enjoyed his old Italian tunes and his grizzly face and his dancing eyes in the fading light of a storied square. I pulled out my sketch pad and paints to catch the Cathedral in that light and realized that, though I had sketched in my travels before, I was not nearly as prolific, nor was it as much fun, as doing it with the boys.

Piazza St Marco

SCENE: THE APARTMENT IN ROME.

(Julia is checking her e-mail as the boys and Lee are preparing a big Saturday night dinner)

JULIA

Honey, the Kramers are going to be in Rome. They'd like to stay with us.

LEE

Who are the Kramers?

JULIA

They said they met us at a party last summer at the Borkawitzes.

LEE

Who are the Borkawitzes?

JULIA

Friends of Nick and Jenny.

LEE

People we don't know, whom we met at a party of other people we don't know, want to stay with us? Nick and Jenny aren't coming. And we *know* them.

JULIA

Uh ... actually they are.

LEE

When are they coming? How come I didn't know that? Do we have room for them?

JULIA

Sure! The kids'll sleep on the floor.

SAM

With their kids. It'll be fun!

LEE

Right.

(He exits quickly to the kitchen)

GABE

Is Dadoo okay?

JULIA

Sure, he just needs time to get used to the idea.

SAM

When are they coming?

JULIA

Tomorrow.

CHAPTER TWELVE

DIECI MINUTI

When you live in a beautiful city like Rome, which has great food and pretty good weather, people are going to visit you. "Oh we just happen to be coming to Rome in two weeks." And add to that the fact that you *want* people to share the place with you. And the boys loved being tour guides. By the time we'd been there a month we'd seen most of the major attractions. Inhaled them in fact. Going to Augustus's palace, which was our neighborhood palace, was like going to movies. We bought the books with photos of the ruined monuments and the clear plastic opposing pages that had them reconstructed as they were. You folded the plastic page over the photo and *eureka*—you got to see the Palace, or the Forum or the Coliseum as it had been two thousand years ago.

Standing on the hill atop Augustus's palace, the boys imagined themselves rulers of the empire, as they waved their cardboard swords and delighted in the arcane facts about their second home.

"I'm Augustus. I rule over a Roman Empire that is larger than it will ever be!"

"I'm Tiberius. I'm living in my villa in Capri, eating fresh figs and prosciutto!"

Then the two of them ran down the crumbling steps at the top of the outlook and into the oval-shaped garden below that had once been Augustus's private race track. They pretended to mount their horses and then chased each other around the two millennium-old track, the capes from their costumes flying in back of them.

When visitors came, the boys were the tour guides supreme.

"This is the only protestant cemetery in Rome. Keats, the poet is buried here. He died in his apartment overlooking the Spanish Steps."

"We've been there. They burned the bed he died in cause he was contagious. So they replaced it with a fake one. It's got a great view. Wanna go?"

Nick and Jenny came with their two girls. And when Julia was out walking one day with their two girls and our two boys, a pair of nuns approached. We'd heard that the population of Italy was decreasing, because, despite the papal edict against it, birth control (and the higher cost of living) had reduced the size of the average Italian family to one and a half children. And here comes Julia walking toward the nuns with four kids. As the Nuns approached, they burst into applause and shouted *"Brava!"*

My sister and brother-in-law, Anne and Jerry, arrived about half-way through our stay. One Saturday morning, while Anne went to find an Italian beauty parlor to have her hair done, Jerry volunteered to join us as we set out on a new adventure. We were going to walk out the Apian way to the catacombs. We were going to walk out the famous Apian Way! It almost gave us the giggles. To be casually saying, "… Well, you take the Apian way to Broadway and hang a left." The idea that a street with this famously ancient moniker was still being used was thrilling. Sure there was a bus to take us out to the catacombs, but we were going to *walk* the Apian way! Ta taaaaa! So the four of us and undaunted Jerry, an ex-marathoner past his seventieth year, set out. We walked through the gate in the old Roman wall and on out "the way." The road begins with cobblestones underfoot and peach-colored little villas flanking it, but soon it no more looks like the Apian Way than any typical road to suburbia. It was a lovely day, and as we now began to see more and more open fields and farmhouses, we wondered, just how far this walk was going to be. The guidebook said it was walking distance. A police car was parked along the road. Two *polizia* were smoking and talking on their cell phones. We'd better hurry. In a moment they'd put on their flashing light, hold up their signal emergency flag, put on their sirens and zoom off ... to lunch. You could always tell when the *polizia* were on a serious mission like ... going to lunch. That's when the emergency flags were held out the window. We approached. "Che distanza il catacombs?" "Ah ... non tropo ... dieci minuti." Oh great...only ten more minutes. No problem. Off we went. Ten, twenty, thirty minutes later, no catacombs! I was beginning to be annoyed. Well, in truth, I was already annoyed, but I now had the courage, or the bad grace, to voice it. "Can't the damned guide books tell you the truth?" or a little more personal, "Who told you this was a short walk from town?" Or real pain in the ass guilt-making, "I never liked graveyards, why do I want to go to one underground? I told you we should have gone to the beach!" Saved—another police car. We waved. He stopped. We approached. "Dove' il catacombs?" The policeman, munching on his roast pepper and eggplant sandwich, (It looked delicious. Where do we get one of those?) pointed the direction we were going, "Diretto. Dieci Minuti!"

"Well, we are going the right direction. It's a shame we didn't bring our sleeping bags." Cold stare from wife. Pitiful looks from children. Positive vibes from Jerry, "Hey it's a nice day. Let's go!" Ok, at least we were going the right direction. Unless ... don't even think it. *But,* it was still ten minutes away. Okay, we can do that. I can do that. Ten minutes later. More fields. Farms. A little village. We stopped for some water. A lemonade. We asked the bar owner the same question. "Ah! Si. Dieci Minuti."

I flipped. The damned catacombs couldn't be ten minutes from *everywhere!* Let's take a cab. Anybody seen a cab? There are buses. I've seen buses. I haven't seen any bus stops but ... Everyone just started walking as I stood there in front of the bar protesting. It's no fun protesting if everyone is walking away. Someone has to listen. I looked at the bar owner and asked in my worst Italian, "Ami il catacombs?" (Do you like the catacombs?) He cocked his head, and said "Non so. Non les vedo" (I don't know. I haven't seen them.) The man lived ten minutes away and he'd never seen them. What was I doing schlepping to them? I ran after the group to inform them that one of the natives hadn't been interested enough to visit his neighborhood catacomb and out of the dust, a police car came hurtling by and we waved and shouted. He stopped. "Si?" "Il Catacombs?" "Dieci Minuti!" We all repeated in unison with him.

A half hour later we arrived. The walk had taken us over two hours. Each time we stopped it was only ten minutes from where we were. How was that possible? Boing! Of course, we realized ... we were talking to Italian policeman. They didn't walk! They didn't walk anywhere! The drove. And they drove like bats out of hell. It took *them* ten minutes! It would take them ten minutes to drive to Venice for God's sake!

The boys laughed uncontrollably. Jerry, whose infectious laugh is gigantic, joined in. My wife too. And then ... I could not help myself. I could crab no longer. It was absurd. It was hysterically absurd. My seven-year-old sons had walked for two hours without one complaint. While the boys were laughing at the idiosyncrasies of the Italian cops, I was moaning and bitching. They had found a way to make the journey work, not only in spite of the messed up instructions, but *because* of them.

Ever after, when we asked directions and the reply stated

that where we were going was not very far. we'd all nod our heads and intone, "Dieci minuti!"

"Dieci Minuti" has now become a kind of code phrase in the family for "always see the information you get in the context of who is giving it!" and a punch line whenever someone tells us something we don't quite believe. When George W. Bush was asked at a press conference how long he expected we would be in Iraq and replied, "Until we've won" we shouted back ... "Dieci Minuti!"

SCENE: STREET, GREENWICH VILLAGE, NEW YORK

(Samuel, Gabriel, and Lee are walking back to the apartment after violin class.)

LEE

Y'know, I loved living in Rome, but what I love about New York? It's *still* a melting pot. Korean fruit stands. Pakistani news stands. Greek coffee shops. Russian cab drivers.

SAM

And us! Natives.

LEE

That's right. You were born here. In Roosevelt hospital. Know what they say is the rarest form of life?

SAM , GABE

What?

LEE

A native in Florida.

SAM

Florida is ugly. It's all new. And boring. Remember when we visited Aunt Anna in Florida?

GABE

She was born in Czechoslovakia .

SAM

Right.

GABE

She survived the holocaust.

SAM

She had an amazing life.

LEE

Yes, she did.

SAM

So why would she move to Florida?

CHAPTER THIRTEEN

THE HOOD

Many years ago, before I had kids, when I was a between-marriages-bachelor, I left my beloved skylighted studio because they raised the rent to an intolerable $240.00 a month. I bought a six room co-op across the street. I was single. Why did I need six rooms? Maybe two rooms for me and four for my dirty laundry? I was approaching my fortieth birthday. I was putting the cart before the horse. I was probably saying to myself, "Okay, you don't have a wife. You don't have kids. At least get a place to put 'em when you grow up!"

But, buying a house is scary. Buying a house makes you instantly a grownup. Overhead! You have to meet a mortgage. Ergo you have to earn a certain amount of money. Yikes. The freelance happy-go-lucky life is over. I remember the first time I bought a house, a little house in Connecticut, I panicked. I asked my lawyer father for advice. "Should I go through with this? What happens if I can't make the payments?" He was terrific. He said, "So, you lose the house." What a surprise. My father was usually Mr. Cautious. And now, like him, I only feel secure when I am financially secure. I realized quite soon that the secret of a happy life was: low overhead! My good friend Danny Klein says the secret of a happy life is: low expectations. Maybe it's both. And being a little bit lucky.

And we were very lucky. When we moved back from Rome, Julia had decided she wanted to start her own literary agency in New York. She had paved the way for this when we lived in L.A., sitting in on informal writers' sessions, where the authors would read pieces they were working on and elicit feedback. Julia's critiques were praised by the writers and excited her about the possibility of doing it further. Back in New York, she interviewed with various literary agencies and was offered several jobs—working on commission. But her desire to be available to pick up the boys after school, and her fabulous chutzpah, "I don't need to work for them on commission. I can learn this business and do it myself!" inspired her to open her own agency. There was a terrific elementary school two blocks away from the apartment and her office. It was all happening in our little neighborhood. We were *damned* lucky. Julia had found her calling, and I had gone for that too big apartment twenty years back—that we'd now all call home.

There is no doubt that I fell in love with Julia because I knew she would be a phenomenal mother. Just as I had found the apartment and projected ahead, "This would hold a family someday," I had felt, "This is a woman to mother a family someday." Of course, it's not as all hard-nosed as that. You fall in love with all aspects of a person. And of a place. But something quite visceral pushes you past reservations you've had to commit to this person. Especially when you've past forty. Life is not endless. There's more to it than being young. There's something big you haven't done. Just because your parents did it and their parents did it, doesn't mean you can dismiss it. Family. It need not be solely the badge of responsibility. Of giving up your youth. It could be, just maybe …an adventure you have been all too blind to embrace.

And indeed it was. And bringing Julia and the boys home to this place, this too-big-for-a-single-man place began not only the anchoring of these family years in "the village," but also a renewed love affair with the city.

The idea of "neighborhood" came from the kids. I'd lived on the same street for twenty-three years before they were born, and I lived in my neighborhood, the Village, without a tremendous sense of belonging all those years. Oh I loved it. Wouldn't live anywhere else. I knew some of the local shopkeepers. But it didn't feel *integral*. Of course, part of this may be me. I find the idea of "belonging" elusive. And I have the feeling that most people feel the same way. Part of it comes with the territory of being a writer. I work alone. And before my family came I was alone most of the time.

When the boys were born, we spent part time in New York. Pushing them around the Village in our double stroller, we found of course that dozens of people would stop us, and stick their faces in the stroller and coo, "Twins?" and then smile and ramble on about their own kids. The boys were stranger magnets. But more important, when we went out with them to shop or to eat, we were recognized in a different way than I was when I lived in the hood alone. People don't forget twin boys. And as they grew up and toddled and walked and especially *talked*, neighbors looked forward to seeing them.

Case in point: when we returned, and the boys were now going to elementary school there, we "discovered" the local coffee shop, Joe Jr.'s, right across the street from the school. I tended toward the dark, villagey cafés. Joe's was a Greek/American coffee shop. Big windows. Vinyl booths. A counter. But because the booths were big, we could all slide in. And we were recognized. And of course, welcomed.

"Hey guys! What are we havin'? Waffles and sausage?"

"French toast."

"And bacon!"

"You got it. Good game last night eh? Another save for Mariano."

"Dadoo said Mariano has more saves than Jesus."

"Whoaaa!"

It became our hangout. And when the boys began going to school, across the street from Joe's, it became their hangout. If, for some reason, we could not pick them up after school, they could go to Joe's and have a snack and wait for us there, and Louie or Gregg or whoever was on duty at the time would take care of them until we arrived. And it's pretty damned good coffee shop food. The fact that the staff there were Yankee fans didn't hurt. Greg got them Joe Torre's autograph. The fact that they knew what we would order before we ordered it made it … well … a club. This began to happen with other merchants. The two old Jewish guys at Jon Vie Bakery knew the boys and always slipped them an extra cookie when they came in. And when we got a dog, oy, it was the only place we knew we could take the dog while we had a coffee and a croissant. So that was another home. Jefferson Market, where I'd gone since I arrived on Ninth Street, became my substitute for the Roman open-air market. Now, back from Rome, Gabe, who has my shopping gene, would come with me to meat counter to stew over what looked best for dinner that night while bantering with the guys.

"What'll it be tonight Gabe? We've got a special on lamb chops."

"Can we afford them, Dadoo?"

"No, but we haven't had them in a long time."

"They're 12.99 a pound! Is that supposed to be special?"

Slowly, but surely, the neighborhood became my neighborhood, because our kids had charmed the merchants when they were tots in strollers. And those merchants had watched them grow up year after year, and we belonged to them, so we became part of their club. Once they were in school, the time to work the neighborhood with them disappeared, but as Julia or I go about our rounds alone now from market to market, we elicit the same interaction we did when the boys were in tow. The normal feeling of being an outsider was dispelled, thanks to our kids, and we now get the full feeling of *living* where we live. Of belonging.

The boys made me feel that this little corner in New York was our place. We were known and welcomed here. It was a small town within the big city. And there were hundreds of them around the city. New York had a bad rep as a cold place. But, living here, especially with kids, treated us to this notion of little cities within the big one.

Sam and Gabe signed up for violin school at School For Strings at Fifty-Fourth and Ninth Avenue. So Julia and I schlepped uptown to take them three times a week.

"Honey, do we have to go all the way up there? Isn't there a school in the Village?"

"This one's the best."

"But ... way up at Fifty-Fourth Street??"

"You won't get a nose bleed."

I just didn't want to leave the hood. I barely left the apartment. We did everything there. We put a curtain rod with a sheet draped over it across the hall and the boys could play volleyball with a spongy soccer ball, a "palla di spuna," that we'd found in Rome. The ceilings were high, so we tried badminton in the living room, but a broken glass lampshade ended that. We made their small bedroom into a submarine, with beds up near the ceiling and desks below, and a basketball net clamped on their closet door. This once-regal Victorian apartment, an uptown pied à terre for nineteenth-century downtown bachelors was being transformed. The apartment that I had been scared to buy, the apartment that was too big for me had filled up with books and toys and robes and pajamas and soccer balls and computers and more books. It had become in many ways funkier than the fourth-floor skylighted walkup I'd cherished so when I was single. It had all the charm and all the warmth and none of the sudden solitude of being alone. It had the neighborhood around it, to which I finally belonged. It had the smell of old wood, and moldy books and simmering bolognese sauce. It had the smell of "family." Something I could not have imagined to have been so precious until it was upon me. So precious in fact that, when we have a crush of guests over for a weekend or a party, when they've left, when the four of us are finally alone sitting around the table, we look at each other and we shout, "Just Family!"

It is an exquisite moment. It is the ultimate club. And no matter how badly we behave we are in it forever.

SCENE: THE KITCHEN OF THE
NEW YORK APARTMENT.

(Sam is doing his homework at the kitchen table. He can hear an argument ensuing in the bedroom. Julia enters the kitchen.)

SAM

What's going on in there?

JULIA

Dadoo and Gabe are having an argument.

SAM

About what?

JULIA

I have no idea. I think sometimes they just like to argue.

SAM

Want me to go in?

JULIA

No, you'll make it worse. You'll take Gabey's side, and Dadoo will flip out and storm out of the room, and then I'll have to calm him down.

SAM

Yeah, but it'll end the argument.

CHAPTER FOURTEEN
THE LAST WORD

I don't know when it began, this preoccupation with having the last word, but I think it was when the boys were about nine or ten. I got into a bit of an argument with one of the boys and then found, when I thought it was over, it wasn't! It went something like this:

"Why did you hit your brother?"
"He called me a stupid jerk."
"You really hit him. He wasn't even looking at you."
"He hurt me by calling me that."
"No matter what he calls you, it doesn't justify hitting."
"Okay, okay, but he's been doing this to me all day. Calling me this."
"Still ..."
"And I was tired of it."
"Okay, but still ... you didn't have to hit."
"Okay, but I wouldn't have hit him if he hadn't said it so often."
"That's no excuse."
"I know, but *that's* no excuse for him to call me names."
"That doesn't make any sense."
"It makes sense to me. He can't call me names."

"Fine. I'll talk to him. But you can't hit him no matter what he calls you."

"Fine. But I only did it because he was doing it a lot."

"No excuse."

" I know, but what's *his* excuse for calling me names?"

And this discussion would still be going on if I didn't leave the room. The point is—my son, *both* of my sons, had to have the last word. A "still" or a "but" had to come after my "That's no excuse," so his statement could be the last one. Why? Because it made him feel somehow that he'd won the argument. Last word equals won. Or something close to winning. Outlasting.

So then the question is, once I realized that this is what he was doing, why did *I* have to add another word to his last word and prolong the agonizing discussion? Because, of course, I, at a distinctly more advanced aged than my son, was caught in the same trap. I wanted to win the damned argument.

The fact that it wasn't a winnable argument did not occur to either of us. My son, wanting to rationalize his actions, had to justify slugging his brother so that , even if he knew he was wrong to do it, he was not at fault!

Say what?

Yes, folks, when the forty-third President of the United States "apologized" for some major screw up by saying, "It was wrong that this happened" as opposed to "*I* was wrong," he was doing exactly what our kids do. He is acknowledging that wrong was done, but can't quite acknowledge that he has a part in the doing. He's saying, "The buck stops ... well ... over there."

It took a few of these discussions for me to realize that I had done the same thing. Until I had to square off with my own kids, I hadn't realized how often I'd acknowledged I was wrong but ... not at fault. There was always a justifiable excuse for my wayward action.

"Julia, did you leave the light on in the bedroom?"

"I was going back there."

"When? You're reading on the living room couch."

"It's one light."

"Electricity is expensive."

"You leave lights on all the time."

"No, I don't, only if I'm going right back into the room."

"I was going back into the bedroom."

"When? Next Christmas?"

"It's a light. It's one light. Shall we talk about your leaving the refrigerator door open all day?"

"That was because the fridge had shifted and the door didn't close all the way. I didn't know that till we found it open."

"I didn't know the light was on until you reported it."

"But, you said you knew and were going back to turn it off."

STOP! Sound familiar? Why couldn't I (a) Just not mention the light? It's no big deal. Julia is as frugal and responsible a person as I have ever known. But my father was a maniac about turning off lights. He'd turn them off while I was *in the room*. Had I inherited his mania? Or (b) Once having made the criticism and having heard her excuse, why couldn't I just let it go? Because, as I saw my sons doing, I had to *win* the argument.

My favorite Julia retort to me was when I walked into the bathroom and noticed a full toilet.

"Who didn't flush?" I yelled.

From down the hall, came Julia's reply, "Get a life!"

I laughed and laughed. She's good.

But I couldn't lighten up with my kids. I had to make sure I had made my point e.g.: "hitting is wrong under any circumstance," and not have them believe that under *this* circumstance it was okay because etc., etc., etc.

But I had forgotten to realize that his wasn't a real debate. My son had heard me. He'd gotten the message, but he still wanted to win the argument so he could feel good, and I had to allow him that, even though it drove me nuts. Allow him the last word because, ultimately, the last word is bunk! The last word is only the last word. Making your point is what matters, and having him understand my point was all that mattered. If I thought he understood my point, then I could allow him the last word, even if it was a silly rationalization of behavior. Even if it, or rather simply, because it made him feel good.

By fighting to win, to beat their dad, I saw how dogged *I* had been, not just as a young boy, but as a goal-oriented, somewhat mature male. And seeing myself, in them, I could now ... let it go, and yes, "get a life."

SCENE: N.Y. APARTMENT

(Boys rush in after school.)

SAM

We're going to try out for the fifth-grade musical—"Guys and Dolls."

LEE

My favorite musical. I saw the original production when I was just about your age.

GABE

You saw the original? Wow.

LEE

Yup. When I was a kid, the Broadway shows did out-of-town tryouts … in Philadelphia before opening in New York. I was sitting way up in the back of the balcony at the Shubert Theatre watching Nicely Nicely sing "Sit

Down You're Rockin' The Boat," and I said, 'That's what I want to do!'"

SAM

Be a gambler?

LEE

Be in the theater. Write a musical like that.

SAM

I'm gonna try out for Nicely Nicely.

GABE

I'm gonna try out for Sky Masterson.

LEE

Wouldn't that be something if you were both in the show that made me fall in love with show business?

GABE

There's only one problem.

LEE

What?

GABE

If I get the part of Sky, I have to kiss a girl.

LEE

What's wrong with that?

GABE

On stage? In front of hundreds of people?

SAM

Come on, Gabe … you don't have to mean it. It's just a play.

CHAPTER FIFTEEN

THE "CLEVELAND RESPONSE"

You *know* that, just because they are twins, they are not alike.

But, knowing that one is more shy, or one is more loquacious, or a dozen little differences doesn't really define their difference. But then something happens that does.

In the fifth grade, at P.S. 41, they were both cast in their senior-year production of *Guys and Dolls*. Sam got the showy role of Nicely Nicely. Gabe got the "cool" lead—Sky Masterson. He was awfully pleased. And as is his wont, he worked awfully hard. We heard them rehearsing their lines, singing their songs in their "submarine room." And on opening night, we "kvelled" in the midst of all the video camera-ing parents and after the show went to hug them to death.

"Gabe, you were great. You were just great. Your sweet, clear voice. We just ... You couldn't have been better."

"Well, I could have been. I got lost in 'My Time of Day' and 'Luck Be a Lady' wasn't strong enough ..."

"We were blown away."

"I'll get better."

Whoops. Gabe's reaction took me back twenty-six years to Cleveland, Ohio. A play of mine was opening at the Cleveland Playhouse, a musical—believe it or not—about the revolution in Czechoslovakia in 1968, entitled *The Prague Spring*. On opening night, after the show, I stood outside, and several audience members came up to me and told me how much they enjoyed the play. To each of them I said something like, "Well, it's not quite there yet. Needs some more work." As I was saying these words, I looked over and saw one of the actors in the play, receiving compliments from another audience member. But the actor was beaming, and saying "Thanks! Great! Glad you liked it! Send your friends!" Instantly I knew that what the actor was doing was enormously attractive. And I was a complete bore. I could not believe what a jerk I was being. And had been for years when, in like situations, people complimented my work. The actor's enthusiastic response to the audience members reinforced their delight in the play. My tepid self-criticisms were saying to the fan, "Well, you may have liked it, but you don't really know what you're talking about!"

I was insulting someone who liked my play. This is not something a playwright can afford to do!

Since that evening in Cleveland I have never ever done that again. I practice the "Cleveland Response." When someone waxes enthusiastic about my work, I reply with equal enthusiasm, starting with "Thank You!" I am enormously receptive. I gush at his or her great good taste. Well, I don't gush, but I sure as hell don't say anything that would in any way dampen their his enthusiasm. Which is exactly what Gabriel was doing then. He didn't know he was doing it. He, in fact, probably felt he was only being honest. I'm sure he was. But he had no idea of the effect it had on those paying him compliments.

Julia would occasionally do the same thing.

"I like that dress on you. You look great."

"I don't know. It makes my arms look beefy."

"Oh, I guess I'm wrong then."

She got the idea. Though it was tough for her sometimes. When I paid her a compliment she learned to just say "Thank you." It didn't necessarily comes easy for her, but, it came—a simple, "Hey, thanks," which really confirmed my love for her and how she looked. Sam, on the other hand, responded to our compliments with, "Yes! Thanks! That was great! I loved it. Thanks!"

Immediately you were buoyed by his enthusiastic response. Some days later I sat alone with Gabriel and asked him why it was so tough to accept a compliment.

"But Dadoo, do you want me to say 'Thank you,' when I think they're wrong?"

"Yes!"

"I can't be a hypocrite."

"You're not being a hypocrite. They loved what you did. They don't care what *you* thought. They want their compliment acknowledged."

"But if I lie, and say 'Thanks' ... "

"You're not lying. They didn't ask what *you* think. They're telling you what *they* think."

"But what if I don't agree with them?"

"This is not the place to disagree with them. They feel good making you feel good. That's all the moment is about. You can't take that away from them by being self-critical."

"It just doesn't feel right."

"It felt weird for me too when I first did it. But I practiced the "Cleveland Response," and I got used to it. It became automatic. And I found, giving back pleasure was very satisfying."

"Being a hypocrite?"

"NO! Being generous!"

I took his face in my hands. "Be generous. Try it. You'll be surprised. You'll feel good doing it.

"Well ..."

"Try it."

It just wasn't easy for Gabey. He was so hard on himself. So self-critical. I couldn't figure out whether he wore it as a badge of honor i.e.: "I'm harder on myself than anyone else could possibly be!" or whether he just didn't have enough confidence to recognize his worth. To acknowledge it. I gave him a big hug. I realized that a ten-year-old boy is *not* going to see the difference between his brother's enthusiastic reaction and his critical one. He's not going to have a Cleveland moment. It took me twenty-six years. I learned that I was going to have to be patient and coach him toward "Cleveland." I learned that it was tough for him, living day in and day out with a super-confident brother. I learned that *I* had to respond to his self criticism with respect, "Gabe, you may have botched a few lyrics in that song. It's great that you want to get better. That you want to be perfect. But ... "

"I know ... I can't rain on their parade."

"Yes."

I gave him a kiss and left him alone in his room. As I walked down the hall, I could hear him singing, "I've never been in love before. Now all at once it's you, it's you for evermore."

(SCENE: BEDROOM OF THE NEW YORK APARTMENT.)

(Lee is packing for a trip to Los Angeles.)

GABE

Dadoo, when you write a play, do you think of the idea first or story first, or the characters first, or what?

LEE

It's different every time.

SAM

The play you're going to do in Los Angeles. Which came first?

LEE

Well, I read an article in a magazine that interested me. The subject matter—but I realized that it wasn't enough for a play. It was just an interesting subject. So .... I had to think of a dramatic situation in which

I could use the subject matter. And characters who would be involved in that situation. That's the hard work. The actual writing is easy.

SAM

Did you do the same thing with the TV series?

LEE

Well, no. The TV series was based on our family life. And the characters were based on you guys and me and mommy. So ... I just had to make it work as a TV series.

GABE

But why didn't it work?

LEE

Well, you know ... there were just too many people, with too many ideas of what it should be, and it lost its integrity.

SAM

What's integrity?

LEE

It's ... like honesty. It's ... like ... well ... If I asked you to do something you didn't believe in. You'd say, "I can't. I would lose my integrity." It's ... the thing that makes the thing ... a special *thing*.

                    SAM

Uh ... huh.

                    GABE

Is your play going to lose its integrity?

                    LEE

I certainly hope not.

                    SAM

If it does, can you find it before we get to see the play??

CHAPTER SIXTEEN

LETTING GO

In May of the year the boys turned ten, a new play of mine, *Defiled*, was produced at the Geffen Playhouse, in Los Angeles. It starred Peter Falk and Jason Alexander and was directed by my old friend Barnet Kellman. I wanted the boys to see it. It would be the first play of mine that the boys had *ever* seen. The only thing they'd seen that I'd written was the TV series. They knew this wasn't my best stuff. They knew that the theater was my first love, but they'd only heard about plays of mine produced before they were born. They knew I did something when I holed up in my study. I was not one of those writers who could not be disturbed. When they came home from school, and my door was open, they knew they could romp in and kibitz, and I'd stop and play. If I was seriously into a scene, I'd close my door to let them know not to disturb me. But then, of course, they'd just open the door and say, "Dadoo, are there any extra bagels from breakfast?" I'd reply, "Honey, I'm working," and then of course came, "I know, but are there any extra bagels?" Fortunately I could weather these distractions and dive back into work. I may have sent the message that Dadoo can't be doing anything too important because he's always available. On the other hand, they got the message that I loved what I did. And it resonated in their own lives.

But in their short lifetime, the only play of mine produced that they could have seen was produced when they were four, at the Williamstown Theatre Festival—a terrific production, but over the heads of four year olds. Even these four year olds. Now, ten, I was sure they'd understand this play, *Defiled*, but I wondered, shouldn't I wait until a production is done in New York? No, that might never happen. Seize the day.

It was also the first time the director, Barnet, and I had worked together since our ill-fated television series. Time may not heal all wounds, but working together on something you love, with little interference from above, heals exquisitely.

The play was about a librarian, Harry Mendelssohn (Jason), who, upset that they were going to remove the old card file system and replace it entirely with computers, threatens to blow up the library unless the files remain. A police detective on the verge of retirement, Brian Dickey (Peter), arrives to dissuade him from this mission.

I had done a rewrite of the play based on a reading we'd had with Peter and Noah Wylie the previous February, and, when we read this new version with Peter and Jason, at the first read through, Peter raised his hand at the end and, almost Columbo-like with one of his patented afterthoughts, he said, "Uh ... The first version I read ... that early version ... that was good. That was just terrific. Golden. Could we ... uh ... could we read that version?"

Barnet took a deep breath. "Peter, why don't we work on this version awhile. See how it goes."

"O—kay. But ... that early version was golden."

For a full week, after each rehearsal, Peter asked again, "Couldn't we just take a look at that early version? It was ... it was ... golden."

Finally Barnet, in hopes of finally putting and end to Peter's daily, insistent requests, said, "Okay. Let's do it. Let's read the early version."

There were moments after I did the rewrite that I thought, "Are these necessary?" The producer is afraid that the play unfolds too slowly? But is he right? Am I forsaking the very integrity I'd lost in the TV series—that I'd championed with Sam and Gabe? I didn't know. Fortunately, in the theater, rehearsing a play, you have *time* to find out. Copies of the earlier version were brought to rehearsal and we read it. All the way through. At its conclusion, Barnet turned to Peter.

"Peter ... You're right. It's better."

And Peter *was* right. Bless his soul. He felt it, and he just kept insisting. I couldn't have done it. I didn't have the clout. But dear, dogged Peter persisted, and we started over with the "golden" version.

Peter's doggedness was not always productive. While Jason sailed through rehearsals, learning his prodigious number of lines easily, Peter scared us. Could he learn all the lines? When the set went up, Peter went onstage and walked around in it. He realized that a step unit (which had only been lines on the floor in the rehearsal room) were going to make some of his action difficult.

"Do we have to have these steps?"

A long drawn out debate ensued. So long that Jason went home. Barnet went home. And finally I was left alone with Peter in an empty theatre. Completely frustrated I finally just said, "Peter, they are not going to spend ten grand to rebuild the set. Get used to it!"

And I went home.

Mr. Falk was brilliant. He never dropped a line. He never tripped on a step. His comic timing was immaculate. Jason, early in the play, showing him the prized architecture of the library says, "This building is so magnificently constructed that you can sit at one end of this room and hear a pin drop at the other." Peter, pauses *perfectly* and says, "Is that good for a library?"

Jason's manic energy and a slowly revealed vulnerability were the perfect foil for Peter's measured professionalism. Watching them slowly, slowly form a bond was delicious. Obviously in a two-character play, the two actors must click. And click they did.

Julia took two days off from work to come out for the opening. When would the boys see it? They had never seen one of their father's plays. And this production was electric. We decided to have them fly out alone, after school ended. Could they fly out alone? (Well, alone with each other.) They'd never done it. We knew kids did it all the time. Sam and Gabe had traveled a great deal with us, but not *without* us. Was I more worried about them coming alone, or coming at all? They were finally going to see the product of all those hours their father spent in his study. They had no idea who Peter and Jason were. That wouldn't impress them. They were coming to see their father's work. I was both excited and nervous. We decided they would fly out for the last performances in July. I met them at the airport, expecting to hear dire stories about "turbulence" and "inedible food," but they ran off the plane laughing, accompanied by a smiling stewardess. I asked her if they were any trouble.

"No, they were a riot!"

Of course, Frick and Frack.

"The pilot let us watch him fly the plane."

These were in the days when that was routine. A friendly pilot would show off the cockpit to kids on board. Gabriel volunteered, "When I grow up I'm going to be a pilot-violinist!"

"How would that work?"

"Well, after the plane is up, and we go on autopilot, I could walk back and play for the passengers."

"Great. I'd fly that airline."

That night they came to the play. They looked at the poster outside. They watched the audience coming in, filling the theater, and leaned to each other to whisper their impressions. I started to breathe a little faster. The play was in good shape. It had been running for two months to full houses. But would *they* like it? Maybe this was a bad idea. I was their father, so they must have figured that I was good at what I did. Why chance it by actually showing them what I did? Why did it matter what they thought. They were ten years old. The play wasn't written for them. It was written for adults. Like the *L.A. Times* critic, who hated it. But the audiences loved it. The adult audiences. What was I doing? This was supposed to be an exhilarating experience. Was I going to over-examine it to death? So, they were ten. They were pretty sophisticated ten-year-olds. They would get it. But how much would they get? The blinking lights in the lobby rescued me from my inane preoccupations. We went in.

There's a magical excitement about a filled theater. The hum from an expectant audience. Of course if you listen to any single conversation, it's sobering. You think they're all going to be talking about your play.

"Honey, did you turn off the oven before we left?"

"I hear Peter Falk plays a detective. Is that all he can do?"

"Y'know, Jason Alexander sings."

"In this play??"

"No. He's been in musicals."

"This is a musical?"

"No, forget it."

It was an incredible set. The main reading room of a soaring old library, the check-out desk, large library tables, and, along the front , old wooden card files were built in under the stage apron. The theatre is a wonderful, old, tudor-style building, and the set designer used that architecture, the actual walls of the theater, as part of the library, so that the entire theater seemed to be an extension of the library itself. The audience was sitting inside the library.

When the play opens, Jason, as Harry the librarian, is checking out explosives he has set up around the library. The phone rings. Jason, picks up the receiver and takes it off the hook. Then from the back of the house, we hear Peter as detective Dickey on a bullhorn, saying that he's coming in … just to talk. He walks down the aisle, entering the library

HARRY

Don't come in here. I'll blow the place.

BRIAN

I'm not armed.

HARRY

Stay back I'll set this off.

BRIAN

I'm here to talk.

HARRY

I don't want to talk. I want action. I'm gonna do it.

BRIAN

Don't do it.

HARRY

I'm going to do it.

BRIAN

Don't. Please, don't.

HARRY

Please? Who are you? Are you with the SOLC?

BRIAN

SOLC?

HARRY

Save Our Libraries Committee.

BRIAN

No, I'm Detective Dickey.

HARRY

A cop.

BRIAN

Yes, but I like libraries.

HARRY

What's the last book you took out of a library?

BRIAN

I don't remember.

HARRY

You don't remember? How long ago was it?

BRIAN

I don't know. Forty, fifty years.

HARRY

The last time you were in a library was *fifty years ago*?

BRIAN

Maybe more.

HARRY

What the hell are you doing here now?

BRIAN

I'm trying to stop you from blowing it up.

HARRY

You? Why do you care? You wouldn't miss it.

BRIAN

You're probably right. But it's my job.

HARRY

What's your job? Saving libraries? They could at least have picked a guy who used one occasionally.

BRIAN

That's not my job.

HARRY

What?

BRIAN

Saving libraries. My job is saving lives. I'm a police detective.

HARRY

When's the last time you saved a life?

                    BRIAN

Day before yesterday.

                    HARRY

Really? Who?

                    BRIAN

Can we talk about your life? Can we talk about what's going on here?

                    HARRY

Who did you save?

                    BRIAN

It doesn't *matter.*

                    HARRY

It matters to me.

                    BRIAN

Hector Rodriguez. He was gonna jump off a bridge.

                    HARRY

Who is he?

BRIAN

He's a painter. An artist. He got rejected at the Art Academy.

HARRY

Like Hitler.

BRIAN

What?

HARRY

If they'd accepted Hitler into art school, millions of people's lives would have been saved. So *shortsighted!*

The boys and I all sat together in the back of the theater in a row set aside for the staff. Gabe, in fact, decided to sit on my lap and as the play unfolded, I sat with my arms around him, while Sam leaned to me, his arm locked in mine. Every so often they'd whisper a question, but by and large they said nothing and moved not at all. Beginning to end, they were caught up in the play and I ... was caught up in holding them while they watched it.

The play is in real time. Ninety minutes. The time is takes for the negotiation. The last book the detective can remember reading was a Hardy Boys book as a kid, and yet he slowly, skillfully burrows into the librarian's life, trying to dissuade him from this radical adventure, by just talking ... talking about himself and how, though not an intellectual, he might understand the young librarian.

BRIAN

When you get older, what you want changes. It's a nice thing actually. You gotta recognize it when it happens. Fast cars are important when you're young. I'm lookin' at retirement in a couple of years. I'm lookin' maybe to go off to Ireland, where my grandfather came from. Go back to the upper reaches of the Liffey River and fish. In God's green country. That's what I want now. That … and to stay alive. My wife's always worried that something's gonna happen to me, cause I'm getting to retirement. She thinks I oughta be doing safer work at my age. It's no picnic being married to a cop. Lyin' to your wife and kids. Wonderin' if some nut's gonna … So, I'd like to go and fish in the Liffey. Isn't there some place you'd like to go?

HARRY

Sure. I'd like to go to Paris. Or to Italy, where I was supposed to go with my girlfriend, but we … I went alone and it was wonderful. But …

BRIAN

So, hey. Go back. That's somethin' to want. That's somethin' you can have. As a matter of fact, that is something I can help you get. Right now. You give all this up … Harry … I'm gonna tell you right now, I will get you a free ticket to Paris or Italy. Take a friend. That's something, huh?

HARRY

You're negotiating.

BRIAN

Yes, yes, I am, but don't take offense. My wife says I do it in my sleep.

As we watched, one boy on my lap, the other cuddled close, the play circled *through them* to me and around in an emotional arc I had never felt before. It's thrilling enough to watch something you've written be exquisitely performed—watch it work, watch it and listen to the audience respond, laugh in all the right places, but the experience is magnified by having your children see what you do and see it done well. It is thrilling beyond belief, because they are thinking, "Oh, this is what Dadoo does alone in his study. He really does something. And not only that, he does it really well."

There is no greater reason to write or create anything than for a moment like this. As I have said, I put off getting married and having children years beyond the normal expiration date so as not to interfere with my creative urges. And here, my children were showing me, with their rapt attention, with their pointed questions after the play, with their obvious thrill at the whole event that—*we* are the reason you do this.

The theater is a cruel business. There is nothing quite as humiliating as opening the newspaper to find a complete stranger savaging something you worked on for years. And then again, nothing as pleasing as another complete stranger delighting in what you'd done. A famous Jules Fieffer cartoon depicts a playwright, going through his history of productions saying, "The critics said of my first play, 'Inept,' 'Drivel.' Both reviews misunderstood my play. The critics said of my second play, 'Pretentious,' 'Abhorrent.' Both reviews totally misunderstood my play. The critics said of my third play, 'A smash hit,' 'A triumph.' Both reviews totally misunderstood my play. They are now misunderstanding to my advantage. In the arts, this is known as success."

Bringing up our children we are constantly misunderstanding each other. But they teach us that we can't panic when we are "panned" as parents by their misbehaviors or rude talk. We have to hang in. And hope, and believe that, if we write the scenario with love and understanding, sooner or later they will appreciate what we've done or, at least, misunderstand in our favor.

From L.A. on, we were not shy about bringing them when a play of mine was performed. No easy task, since the next two productions were in Tokyo!

Defiled was performed there in Japanese. An agent from Japan, Martyn Naylor, a British gentleman who still wore a monocle, happened to have seen the Geffen production and said in charmingly old-world manner, "Hmmm, yes ... well ... the

Japanese will like this. It's about something." And so, a year and a half later, the Japanese Producer, Mr. Eguchi flew us out, the entire family, to see his production. We were given hotel rooms and wined and dined and treated like royalty. And best of all, the production was superb. It was in Japanese, we knew it was good. The boys and Julia sat in the theater with the play in their laps, keeping up with it in English, but even without knowing the language, a good production has an integrity that is projected beyond the words. Not something a playwright would readily admit. In another language it becomes something else. And can work just as well … in another way. The boys understood that, as we gathered after the play.

"I stopped looking at our script after awhile, Dadoo, and it was really good anyway."

"And it was so different from Los Angeles. That's really interesting."

That summer we all saw an old play of mine *Breakfast with Les and Bess* in French, in a production in Montreal. Now they were becoming old-pro critics.

"I know it was in French, Dadoo, but don't you think it was too jokey?"

"You mean, broad?" I replied, "Well they played it as farce. I liked it."

"I don't know."

They were learning about interpretation. And about letting go. Once I've finished a play, after the first run, when someone wants to do it and I'm not there, they pretty much can do it as they please. Not necessarily the way I imagined it. It's kind of fun to see if it still works. And good play will. I remember when I was a kid, seeing a summer stock production of *Death Of A Salesman*. An awful amateur production. But the play was so solid … it still worked. Sometimes, something you create will come out even better when it's reinterpreted. Other people's imaginations combined with yours can take it somewhere new. Attention must also be paid to this.

The boys were only ten, but I could see them soaking this all up. And already beginning to understand the tricky vicissitudes of creating anything.

And I began to understand that someday I would have to let *them* go. And they would develop in ways that I had not imagined, but that, hopefully, because Julia and I had infused them with the values of hard work and love of adventure and the sacred closeness of family, that they would use these as a grounding to become something different enough from us and from each other.

SCENE: THE LIVING ROOM OF THE
NEW YORK APARTMENT.

(It is 2:00 a.m. on election night, 2000. Gabriel, ten, and Lee are up watching the returns on TV. Julia and Samuel have gone to bed.)

TV

It's too close to call.

LEE

Come on, Gabey you have school tomorrow.

GABE

I'm staying up.

CUT TO: The living room, forty five minutes later. 2:45 a.m.

TV

... and George W. Bush has been declared the winner

and will become the forty-third President of the United States.

(Lee hits the remote and turns off the television. He turns to Gabe to lead him to bed. Tears are rolling down Gabe's face. Lee comes to him. Hugs him)

LEE

Oh, Gabey.

GABE

It's not fair. He stole it. He stole Florida. The ballots are faulty. They stopped black people from voting. He stole it!

LEE

Maybe he did. Maybe not. We'll find out more later.

GABE

It can't happen here. It can't happen, can it?

LEE

I hope not. Let's ... go to bed.

(Lee takes Gabriel's hand and leads him down the hall to bed, tears still in his eyes)

CHAPTER SEVENTEEN

WAKE UP, MR. PRESIDENT

We were and are a very politically involved family. When the boys were two, they had their first election party. They watched the returns and cheered Clinton's victory. And again in '96. In 1998, we were driving to the house in Massachusetts when we had to turn the radio off, because the newscaster was reading the transcripts of Bill Clinton's impeachment trial and Samuel asked, "What's fellatio?"

We watched Al Gore nominated, on a satellite television on a remote island on the Quebec river in Canada. We watched the debates, as George Bush grinned and preened and mispronounced the names of foreign leaders and Al Gore seemed to be talking to everyone as if he were reading them a chapter from *The Cat in The Hat*.

It was inconceivable that Bush could win. As bad a campaigner as was Gore, Bush's oozed incompetence. And yet, he had "won." The results were suspended for weeks. The recount started. And was stopped by the Supreme Court. And *Bush v. Gore* went before the Court.

Every day during the trial, Gabey came right home after school and sat in front of the TV and watched.

"Boise is not asking the right questions! He's not tough enough."

"He's a top attorney Gabe. He teaches at Yale. Maybe this is his tactic."

"Gore should have just asked to recount Brower County. Not the whole state. They've got to attack the fraud in that county, and then the validity of the whole state will collapse."

Truth be told, I think Gabey would have done a better job than Boise. But ten-year-olds are not allowed to argue before the Supreme Court. Sam cynically dismissed the whole thing.

"The fix is in. The court has a republican majority, Gabey, why are you watching all this?"

But he did. Every day. Just as I had rushed home from school in 1954 to watch the Army-McCarthy hearings. McCarthy was evil incarnate in our family, and even as a teenager I knew when Joseph Welch, the attorney for the Senate committee, intoned to the sweaty, stoic, jowly cheeked McCarthy, "Have you no decency, Senator? At long last have you no sense of decency?" that something important had happened. That something had turned. And I had seen it.

But I had seen something *positive* happen. Gabriel was watching the fabric of our democracy rip apart as the Court voted along party lines to prevent a Florida recount and elect George Bush, despite the fact that he'd lost the popular vote.

Gabey was disconsolate. For days.

"How could O'Connor do that? How can you vote along party lines at a time like this?"

"Maybe she felt it was best for the country to have the election settled. Not to drag it out."

"That irresponsible. What's good for the country is a fair election. That's completely irresponsible!"

Gabriel was angry and bewildered and disconsolate for days. He just didn't know how to absorb what had happened. It wasn't supposed to happen here. In this country. We could get bad presidents. The wrong guy could win. That happened, but to have someone elected who didn't win the popular vote, then win by possibly fraudulent tactics, threw him. Absolutely threw him. He walked on sea legs for weeks. His stomach was upset. He slept badly and was angry about everything.

"My civics class is silly."

"Sam eats too loud."

"Dadoo's sandwiches are boring!"

"I hate my bed!"

"This country's a joke. We're a joke. The whole world is laughing at us. We're a joke."

Gabriel had faced a myriad of small disappointments in his young life, from not being good enough to play T-ball to missing his favorite float in the Macy's parade. Small stuff. This was different. This floored him. Why? It wasn't because his candidate lost. It was because it wasn't *fair*. Fairness is everything to a child. There's losing a game and there's losing a game unfairly. There's getting a bad grade and getting one unfairly. And for someone like Gabe, with rigorous standards for himself, when the standards for the our whole system of government fail, in a country built on the supreme fairness of its system, then he's completely at sea. He was angry, and he just didn't know what to do with his anger. And I didn't know how to help him.

Samuel took his anger and turned it into a musical. Yes, he wrote a musical about George Bush. I had once told him the old joke about how the British were so egocentric, especially at the height of the empire, that they derided everything French. They would say, "You know of course, if you wake a Frenchmen up suddenly, in the middle of the night, he speaks perfect English."

Samuel wrote a musical called *Wake Up Mr. President*. Here are some snippets:

TV MODERATOR

Hi, Welcome to the Wake Up Debates, where we wake up the candidates from a sound sleep to find out what they really think. We have moved the presidential candidates, Mr. Raymond Poodleneck and Governor Harvey Hardhat, and their beds to the studio, so we can wake them up and ask them questions. Wake up Harvey! Wake up Raymond!

(They wake up)

The first question from the audience goes to Mr. Poodleneck.

AUDIENCE MEMBER

What do you think should be done about health care?

RAYMOND

(Yawns) I can't think. I'm tired. I wanna go back to bed. Where's my Teddy bear?

MODERATOR

Mr. Hardhat, what's your response?

RAYMOND

I'm for free health care.

MODERATOR

But you're a republican. Who's going to pay for it?

RAYMOND

The democrats!

Then after a controversial election, in which Florida would decide the winner, Katherine Harris, famous for her *Bush v. Gore* decision, is again called on to "help" Mr. Hardhat win. And the CNN moderator sings this song .

Oh, Katharine Harris is a mean one.
She is no fun.
She helped Bush win the Sunshine State
When he was not the rightful winner.
That was not very great.
Now I wanna skin her.

Oh, that evil stare,
We better beware,
So I Declare.

Oh, Katharine Harris, how could you
Have Bush win,
When it wasn't true?

Samuel went on to write many more songs. A whole musical, in fact, that was performed in high school, with the sophisticated lyrics of a seventeen-year-old. But this scene, written by a ten-year-old equally upset as his brother at the outcome of the election, was his way of directing the anger and disappointment he felt. For him, it was absurd. Sam had taken his fury and redirected it into a creative burst.

Gabe couldn't do that. And we couldn't help. Gabe felt the disappointment personally and could not compute it in what had been the safe, ordered world of his life. There is only so much you can do as a parent. You cannot prepare your children for certain major disappointments. It's been said that you are only as happy as your least happy child, but I think also that you're only as good a parent as you are to your neediest child.

Gabe taught us that you can't solve every hurt. And frankly, I don't think they expect you to. They just want you to be their constant. The thing that does work when other things fail. The thing that loves them no matter what. And allows them in the comfort of their family to come to terms, at their own speed, with the inconsistencies of the real world. The little things you do to create this safe world—the nightly kiss in bed, the staying up all night to help with their homework, the letting them pick the Christmas tree, the very one they want, as long as it takes—these things are what get them through the tough times. Not your advice. Especially when you don't have any.

SCENE: THE KITCHEN IN THE
NEW YORK APARTMENT.

(Samuel and Gabriel are putting the Chanukah candles in the menorah.)

SAM

Daddo, we celebrate Chanukah and Christmas, and Passover and Easter... Is it okay to celebrate every holiday?

DADOO

Sure. Celebrations are good.

GABE

Are there any holidays we don't celebrate?

DADOO

Chinese New Year.

GABE

Why?

DADOO

We're not Chinese.

SAM

We're not anything. We're just half of everything.

DADOO

You don't have to *be* something to celebrate a holiday. The celebration itself is a reason to celebrate it.

SAM

So we *can* celebrate Chinese New Year.

DADOO

Sure! Look up the date. And when it comes, we'll go to Chinatown.

JULIA

We're going to Chinatown? We're having Chinese food for Chanukah?

(The boys giggle uncontrollably.)

CHAPTER EIGHTEEN

YES, THERE IS A SANTA CLAUS

In September of 2001, the boys has just started Middle School in New York when the World Trade Center disaster occurred. I was at the YMCA at Twenty-Third Street when I saw the planes hit on television. Walking home down Sixth Avenue, I saw the burning towers. Crowds filled the street. I felt it ghoulish to just stand there and watch, so I went into the market near my corner to shop. A few minutes inside, I heard a loud shriek from the crowd. I ran outside to see the first tower collapse. My stomach turned over. I went home. I called Julia. She was watching at work. We called the boys' school. There was a lock-down at school. Julia and I went up to Twenty-First Street to pick the boys up. We explained to them what had happened and kept them from watching it over and over again on TV. That night the restaurants and cafés in the Village were jammed. No one wanted to be alone.

The next day, September 12 was our anniversary. We went to our favorite Italian restaurant to celebrate and to distract ourselves. After dinner, walking home, I sniffed the air. It was acrid.

I could smell smoke. People on the street were wearing masks. The wind had shifted. For the previous thirty-six hours it had blown the burning Trade Center rubble east, toward Brooklyn. Now it was blowing north, up the island. We had no idea what toxic stuff was in that wind. I turned to Julia and the boys, "We're getting out of here—now."

We were lucky. We could leave. We packed and carried our stuff to our car on Twenty-Fourth Street and drove to the mountains in Massachusetts, and spent the rest of the week, numbed, but safe, in the clear Berkshire air.

Over the next two months, Gabriel had night terrors. He would wake up in the middle of the night wailing, and we would rush into his room and find him perched on the edge of his elevated bed about to jump or fall. We'd help him down and walk him down the hall as he thumped his feet and shouted incoherent phrases. We sat him down in the living room and talked to him quietly, trying to ease him up, rather than wake him suddenly, which was the prescribed cure. Once awake, I'd often calm him down by having him recite the starting Yankees lineup, which took his mind off his nightmares and began to relax him. Sometimes we'd turn on the TV and find a movie, hopefully a musical that would take him to a happier world. One night, we turned on the TV at two a.m. and came in on the Howard Stern show. He had three strippers on and was holding a quiz show. Why we didn't change the channel, I don't know, but we watched as Howard asked a frizzy blonde in sequined pasties, "How many states are there in the USA?" She bit her lip, thought for a moment and then said, "Um ... fifty six?"

Gabe was awake. He howled with laughter. He has a very contagious laugh. It rises up the scale as he giggles uncontrollably. We all laughed, as much at Gabey laughing as at the show. And all the fears that engendered his nightmare vanished in the silliness of the moment.

Gabe couldn't wait till morning to tell Sam about the strippers.

"She didn't even know how many states there were." And he laughed again at the memory of it. Sam spun to us at the breakfast table.

"Hey, can I watch it tonight?"

On Thanksgiving day, we took the boys uptown to watch the Macy's Parade. Would floating Snoopy and waving Santa break the pall? It seemed to help. We bundled up in a chilly, misty rain, warmed by a thermos of hot chocolate and cheered our favorite balloons and bands.

It was going to be okay, we thought, and we prepared for Christmas as if it were any other year.

But would it be the same? The boys were eleven years old now. They'd been writing letters to Santa as long as they could write. Would the tragedy in September and their advancing age have a sobering effect? Would they tell us, "We're not writing this year? We know. We know he doesn't exist. It's all make believe. We felt our world was safe. It's all make believe."

"Mommy, Dadoo, do you think it's too late to write to Santa?" Samuel chimed in a week before Christmas.

We were surprised and enormously pleased.

"Of course not!"

"We don't want anything," Gabe added. "But we've written every year, and he might be disappointed if he didn't hear from us."

"Or worry!"

"Or worry!"

It was odd how delighted we were. We knew that someday—some Christmas—they were going to say to us that we didn't have to bother with the Santa Claus thing. But we were glad it was not yet. Not this Christmas. The letter to Santa was always written at the last minute, sometimes as late as Christmas eve, and then rushed to the local post office to be forwarded to Santa. There was never any panic that Santa wouldn't have time to give what they requested for Christmas, because the boys never asked for anything. They used the letter, basically to schmooze with Santa, because—here's the beautiful part—Santa always replied in kind.

He responded in detail to their letter. Who was this "Santa" who wrote back? A few questions in town and we discovered that it was our local West Stockbridge Massachusetts postman, Mike Perkins. He would intercept all the letters to Santa, read them, and answer every single one on the Santa stationary he had had made up. It did not matter how late you wrote, or how much you wrote, he always replied. It was one of the singularly magical things about small-town life. The first time we wrote to Santa, we just sent the letter off to "Santa, North Pole," and thought, well, that was it. When Jim's first letters came back, with an expansive reply to each of the boys, we were stunned. The next year, the boys were so excited to have gotten a personal letter, replete with references to their love of the Yankees and their violin lessons and their sledding adventures that the new letters were filled with even more life details. Little by little, year after year, the letters became a substitute for a year-end diary. They were multi-paged tomes. The boys would spend a whole day writing their Santa letters. And even when, as we knew they must, they reached the age when they couldn't still believe in Santa, they dedicated themselves to writing.

"He'll be bummed out about the Yankees blowing the World Series."

"On a bad throw by Mariano."

"He's a big Yankee fan."

Because public schools never let out until sometimes the day before Christmas, the tree was often bought on Christmas eve. "Fresher" we rationalized. We drove up from New York and went to the local Berkshires tree farm, where, on alternate years, odd for Sam, even for Gabe, the boys got to pick out the tree. 2001 was Sam's year.

"Choose a tree already Sam!"

"Gabe, it's my year. You took forever last year. I'm going to find the perfect tree!"

"It's getting dark. And it's cold."

"I don't care."

We hadn't worn proper boots. The field was shin-deep in snow. It was cold. It was getting dark. The only one enjoying the drawn-out process beside Sam was our new dog, Teddie. She was a "rescue dog"—an abandoned dog we'd found on line. A chow-golden mutt. She was having a ball chasing the tree farmer's dog through the snow.

"Sam I'm fareeeezing!"

"Do you like this one?"

"Yes."

"Yes."

"YES!"

After the tree trimming, after they were finally upstairs and tucked in bed, Julia and I snuggled in bed with them and I read them "A Visit from Saint Nicholas." To spice up the story each year, I read each stanza in a different accent— even though most of my accents devolved by the end of the stanza into Yiddish. "Now, desh avay, desh avay, desh avay all!"

After I finished the reading, after we turned the boys' light out and heard them talking excitedly to each other in bed, Julia went down to finish wrapping, but I wanted to be alone for a moment. I just went into our bedroom and sat down on the bed. I couldn't get the thought out of my mind: what a wonderful myth the Santa Claus story is. All religions had been built on myths of some kind. Who knows what really happened to Moses in the desert, or for that matter Christ on Calvary? There is no doubt in my mind (and most scholars') that the biblical renderings of the lives of everyone from Abraham to Paul were enriched and embellished to not only entice followers to the fold, but to make a better story out of a good story. Whether the Red Sea actually parted or not as rendered by CB DeMille is not important. The Jews were saved from the Pharaoh. You want to save them by having Pharaoh die of a stroke or do you want the Red Sea to part and swallow up his army as he looks on in awe? Spin is not new. The origins of all the major religions were spun. For good reason. Even if everything that happened in the bible is true, it still can be made more exciting. Religions were never sold on their intellectual integrity. Most people could not read. Stories were told and passed on by those who could. And written by those who had a stake in the success of the religion. Good story-telling was captivating. Before we knew about quantum physics and the big bang, the idea that Eve talked to a snake in the Garden of Eden, ate a forbidden piece of fruit (a quince, updated to apples for the Western audience), and was banished from paradise is heartbreaking. Give her a chance! She was hungry! She had no idea that snakes are supposed to talk! What was so bad about being naked? It was warm there. Embarrassment had not been invented. There was no one around to invent it. And anyhow, sooner or later she and Adam had to have sex (sin!) if there were gonna be any more people to follow the word of God. It doesn't all add up. But it doesn't have to. It's good story-telling. Read Grimm's fairy tales. People are constantly disobeying orders (See: Red Riding Hood) and getting into trouble. It's nail biting! And then they are punished. "Oy!" we say, or some of us say, "Weren't you told not to go into the woods, kid? The secret of good story-telling is putting your main character in trouble. Having him or her do the wrong thing, so you can say, "Don't do that!" and then watching himthem try to squirm out of trouble, or not, or pay for his/their misdeed the rest of their life/lives. Jack disobeys his Mom. Sells the cow for some stupid seeds. The beanstalk grows. Don't climb it. He climbs it. Run from the Giant. He slays the giant (of course). He does everything wrong and comes out right. Religion is built on stupid mortals doing everything wrong and coming out right. Because ... because God is with them. It's great. He's great.

The Christmas myth is based on kids being absolute terrors all year long and having a chance to redeem themselves by promising Santa that they will be good next year. OR, if they've been good all year, being rewarded for that. It's a no-lose situation. My favorite kind. I wrote down all of these thoughts.

I realized that what we learned from our kids was the shibboleth I'd been taught as a playwright: *the willing suspension of disbelief.* It's essential to the theater, but as a writer, you don't consciously think about it while you're writing. In many ways, you think the opposite. You think, Will the audience buy this? Do I have to be *more* consistent? Are my characters and their actions consistent. Consistent. Consistent. Consistent. But life is not consistent. It's a cauldron of contradictions. Sounds like a title: *Harry Potter and the Cauldron of Contradictions*. I wish I had a dollar for every critique of every play I'd written chiding me for the inconsistency of my characters. "But," I would plead, "an insecure woman *can* be tough. She *acts* tough to cover her insecurity. Or, a moralist *can* be a hypocrite. See any number from, Henry Kissinger to Newt Gingrich. But the point ... the point is ... after being taught that I *can,* exploit the audience's desire to believe anything they see on stage, I get conservative. Cautious. *Naaa, they won't believe this. Consistency is all.*

Well, my kids were anything but consistent with other kids their age. As they grew up, nine, ten, eleven, they *continued* to believe in Santa Claus. Every year they wrote him letters. We never told them that the postman was writing back. It was always Santa! Even though we happened to go to the post office every year after Christmas so the boys could fete Mike with a violin duet. It wasn't *quid pro quo* for Santa's letter. It was just ... what we did. And every year we hung the stockings and put out the presents after they'd gone to bed. And let them put out a glass of cider and cookies for Santa. And I would spread ashes from the fireplace on the floor, even leave a footprint to indicate his having come. And every year most of the presents were "from Santa." And every year I read, "A Visit from Saint Nicholas."

Okay. So your child reaches eleven, twelve, and you think, "Come on, they can't still believe." But you are waiting for *them* to say, "Mom, Dad, you can cut out the Santa stuff. We know." They don't say that. They write to him. They put out the cider and cookies. The whole routine. Say nothing. So ... *we* say nothing. We say, "Maybe they love the idea of Santa so much that they are believing beyond their years." Or, we wonder, "Have they stopped believing, but are afraid to tell us, because we'd be disappointed?" Hey, who's the parent here? Or are they now masters at the willing suspension of disbelief? Do they know the truth (well, a truth) and have so willed themselves not to succumb to it that they believe the myth? Why not? Again, every major religion is built on that foundation. I may call it the willing suspension of disbelief. Most folks call it faith.

I always wondered why the smartest professor I had in college was a Catholic convert. A convert? He knew better and converted to this? How does an intellectual do that? I never asked him, but witnessing my kids' extended belief in Santa Claus into their thirteenth and fourteenth years, I figured very simply: it makes them happy. It made my prof happy. It was comforting. It was neat! Santa's neat. Why give him up? And so they didn't.

And three years later, based on my notes from that 2001 Christmas eve, I sat down to write a play about an astronomer, whose son decides not to believe in Santa Claus, so upsetting him that *he* begins believing. The astronomer's steadily dedicated belief in Santa, a reaction he says to 9/11 and his rage against organized religion, but more likely a reaction to his son's growing up too fast and his attempt to prevent it, was anything but consistent with his past behavior. He was an inordinately sane man. His wife, unsure of that, sends him to a shrink, who senses that the astronomer's, Howard's, new belief may be an escape from the anger in his real life.

DR. WEISSWASSER

What are you angry at?

HOWARD

I'm angry at my wife for insisting I come here.

DR. WEISSWASSER

Uh, huh. Anything else?

HOWARD

I'm angry at God for not existing.

DR. WEISWASSER

Uh, huh.

HOWARD

I'm angry at myself for disappointing my son.

DR. WEISWASSER

Uh, huh. Could you expand on that?

HOWARD

I'm angry at F.D.R. for not bombing the trains that took the Jews to the concentration camps.

DR. WEISWASSER

On your self anger. Could you …

HOWARD

I'm angry at the Dodgers for leaving Brooklyn. I'm angry at the French for being angry.

DR. WEISSWASSER

Could you …

HOWARD

I'm angry at a helluva lot of things. We'll be here all day.

DR. WEISSWASSER

Could we concentrate on your self-anger.

HOWARD

Why?

DR. WEISSWASSER

It's ... It may be at the root of your malaise.

HOWARD

My anger is at the root of my malaise? That's backward! My malaise is at the root of my anger!

DR. WEISSWASSER

Fine. Why?

HOWARD

Why what?

DR. WEISSWASSER

Why do you have a malaise and why does it make you angry?

HOWARD

If you had a malaise wouldn't it piss you off?

DR. WEISSWASSER

Not ... no it would ... cause me to examine myself and wonder why I was unhappy.

HOWARD

I'm not unhappy. It's a malaise. I'm depressed.

DR. WEISSWASSER

But you're not unhappy.

HOWARD

No, I'm angry, because I'm a happy person who is depressed. If I was an unhappy person who was depressed, it would all make sense and I wouldn't be angry.

(the doctor just looks at him)

Is this too arcane for you?

The shrink is unwilling to believe that a sane adult could believe in a child's myth. But, I had been so seduced by my own son's willing belief in something unbelievable for whatever reason (to please us, to comfort them) that I became a believer too, if not wholeheartedly in Santa's existence, then at least in his principles. And in the idea that I, as a writer, could make an audience believe in a man who believed in a child's god.

The boys, to this day have never fessed up to not believing in Santa. The words, "OK, enough with the stockings and the cookies … we *know*," never came.

Whether it's the love of the ritual that keeps alive their childhood or whether maintaining the belief is as fun for them as it is for us, we don't know. We just do it.

And every year, so far, the boys write to "Santa." They are

seventeen at this writing. Will they continue writing next year and the next, when they are in college? Has Santa ever gotten a letter from a college student? All I know is, if they write to Santa, Mike at the Post Office will write back. And, I will make copies of their letters to him and his replies and save them—the detailed memories of the year they have lived. They are memoirs disguised as letters to Santa. Cogent and revealing and magical.

What I learned from my children was that, when life is good, we need to exult in it with someone besides friends and family, someone who is as mysterious as life itself. And when things are dark, we have to find a way to make ourselves happy. Santa was their way. They needed to believe. And so they did.

SCENE: THE NEW YORK APARTMENT.

(Sam is practicing violin. Julia is accompanying him on the piano. Sam makes a mistake. Stops. His arms drop. He screams in frustration. Takes a deep breath. Turns to Julia.

                    SAM

Mommy, knock, knock.

                    JULIA

Who's there?

                    SAM

Phillip Glass.

                    JULIA

Phillip Glass who?

SAM

Phillip glass.

JULIA

Phillip Glass who?

SAM

Phillip Glass.

(Sam starts to giggle)

JULIA

Phillip glass who?

SAM

Phillip glass, Phillip glass, Phillip Glass …

(Sam falls down on the floor laughing. Julia turns on the piano bench. Then leaps on top of him and kisses him and tickles him as he howls.)

CHAPTER NINETEEN

SOOTHING THE SAVAGE BREAST

It is spring. A muggy New York day for May. We are sitting in the little recital hall at School for Strings, waiting for Samuel and Gabriel, just having turned thirteen, to perform the Bach Double Violin Concerto.

The boys have been taking violin lessons for eight years. We have heard them go through their repertory since they first began playing back in L.A., in 1995. We have heard "Twinkle, Twinkle Little Star" and "Go Tell Aunt Rhody" and "Windsong." We were lucky in that their first teacher was not a strict Suzuki teacher who restricted them to playing on the E string for an entire year. After a few weeks of that I fear I would've put my head in the oven (just to deaden the sound). But they learned to play a host of sweet tunes. Over and over and over. They learned enough basic fingering to play half a dozen songs, and though they played them roughly, they *played* them. They were actually playing violin. And they were excited. Motivated to play more songs. And more songs better. They were hooked. And now, eight years later, they were about to play Bach.

The recital begins with the youngest players playing first. Boys and girls the same age that Sam and Gabe were when they started. Some have barely started, indeed just stand before the audience in their Sunday best, hold the violin and, to the accompaniment of the ever popular "Twinkle," saw back and forth on the E string. The idea is to get them used to performing before an audience. To relax them so that, when they're older, they won't be susceptible to stage fright—they will be pros and be above it. As the kids play, I glance over at Sam and Gabe. They don't look relaxed. Julia takes a deep breath and looks down at the program. The boys are next to last. A long wait.

You have to have enormous patience to allow two five-year-olds to learn the violin at the same time. The practices do not fill your home with what can be called a pleasant sound. Sam especially screeched unmercifully. Gabe had a deft touch ... and even then, his tone, with the limited repertoire was clear and soft, but there comes a point when you just want to shout, "OK, enough Twinkle already!" But you can't. Your children are being groomed to someday play at the Hollywood Bowl. Carnegie Hall. Lincoln Center. Well, OK, this does not really enter your mind. Especially hearing the Jack Benny-like tones coming out of their tiny instruments. You justify it by saying, "So, maybe they won't be violinists, but this is good for them. It's a challenge. Challenges are good." Yes, but it was a challenge for us too. You try to fantasize. To project forward ten, fifteen years to when they might play Mozart, or Kreisler ... but ... you can't. You just hear "Twinkle." And you grit your teeth and wonder why they couldn't have played something easier like ... the flute ... or something less grating like ... the French horn. Violins are really hard to play. Pick one up. Try it. The violin is held so that it's difficult to see what you're playing. It's under your chin, and it's up in the air to one side. You have to press your fingers on different strings in different *unmarked* places to get different notes. And,

and ... *at the same time* you have to drag the bow across these strings, different strings for different notes, to somehow actually play a tune. It's the old, "can you walk and chew gum at the same time?" routine. This is more like, can you walk, chew gum, juggle three balls, sing and drink a soda at the same time? Neophyte violin players are helped by the fact that the stem of the violin is marked by strips of tape to help them find the notes, but it still ain't easy. Yet they were undaunted. I was daunted. They were un. And as they played more music, they listened to more music. Especially violin music. They understood what they were striving for. They listened to Perlman, and Haifitz, and Shaham—had a glimmer that if they worked hard enough, someday that same sound would come out of their violins. Learning the instrument, they fell in love with the music.

At School for Strings, the littlest kids are finished performing and we are moving into the eight-, nine-, ten-year-olds. Some have enormous presence and no tone. Some look awkward, but play smartly. We can see in them our children growing up before our eyes. The five- and six-year-olds screeching out primitive tunes. The pre-teens testing themselves with Handel and Haydn. We watch their parents, leaning slightly forward when they play, rooting them on, as if they were on the sidelines at a little league game. A chubby little Japanese girl, probably only six, knocks Handel out the park! Whoa! You can see all the waiting kids, looking at each other, intimidated. We have to follow that?

I had given up my childhood clarinet because it was too hard, and now my children were pursuing a much more difficult instrument. Well, they might understand my giving up if they'd heard me *play* the clarinet. I did play it through college. And in my brief stint in the army. I even got a weekend off from basic training in the army so I could go home and get my clarinet in order to play in the company band. You had to hear our company band to believe it. Two saxophones, a clarinet, a drum and a flute. No trumpets. It sounded like a wounded animal sighing. And the leader of the band was a Polish expatriate who would exhort us to play "Hank is Away." We'd all look at each other: "'Hank is Away'? What song is that?" Then he'd hum some of it, and we'd understand. "Ahhh, Anchors Away!" It was my last gig.

The boys would not hear of surrendering. Why should they? Along the way they kept getting positive reinforcement. When we lived in L.A., we went down to La Jolla to visit my old buddy and summer camp mate (we'd known each other then almost fifty years) and the boys took their violins. Out on Bobby and Lorna's patio, they did a little concert. They played, "Lightly Row," or one of their simple repertoire, on a quiet afternoon, while my old friend and his wife listened indulgently. When they finished, I looked over at Lorna and saw tears in her eyes. It's not that they played well, which they had, but these tiny creatures had just invested so much into these complex instruments and gotten such a sweet sound to come out. And they were so serious. And so unafraid. It moved to tears.

In the recital room, the children are getting older, bigger. And playing better. With some exceptions. One skinny, rosy-cheeked young girl just loses her place. A big sigh, she stops, looks at the accompanist helplessly. They confer. She backs up and starts again. A young blonde boy, built like a linebacker, surprises everyone by playing a sweet and delicate waltz. We look down at the program. Sam and Gabe are next.

The boys file in from "backstage" and stand in front of the piano. They are wearing their blazers and bow ties and the other parents smile at the sight. A woman to my left leans to me, "How nice they look. Kids just don't dress up any more."

"Thank you."

"They tie their own bow ties?"

"Not yet. Bach is easy. Bow ties are hard!"

They tune their violins. Gabe just can't get his right. His

teacher, Katherine, comes, takes the instrument, makes an adjustment and hands it back. He strokes it himself. Nods to Sam and the accompanist. Okay. Julia and I take a deep breath. Sam and Gabe take a deep breath and begin. They are playing Bach! My hero. The father of twenty children and the composer of the resounding "Christmas Oratorio" and the heart rending "Air for G String." There is nothing he could not do. And that wonderful, weird, warm, tingle goes up my back as I fully grasp that *they are playing him.* A duet is unusual for a recital. It's usually only solo pieces, but their being twins made this exception happen. If you make a mistake as a soloist, you recover and go on. You make a mistake in a duet, it's like a small train wreck. A contrapuntal crash. They have memorized the piece. All students must. More tension to the mix. My stomach tightens as they begin. They progress without a glitch, and my stomach relaxes, and the feeling flies up into my chest. How long ago had it been to that patio in La Jolla where they were playing "Lightly Row?"

I truly could not grasp the idea that they were my children. That my silly little sperm, sperms actually, had fertilized my wife's eggs and brought forth two Bach-playing violinists. Were the sperm encoded? Did they "talk" to each other on the way up the vaginal canal?

"Hey ... this is *my* trip. Back off."

"Yours? This is my only chance, I'm gonna get outta here too!"

"Oh? You ... uh ... You interested in music?"

"Oh, yes, I love music. It's in my genetic makeup."

"Your what?"

"If I have it, you have it."

"Oh yeah? Great. So ... if we make it ... I mean if we, y'know, fertilize and come to term and all that, whatdaya think about maybe playing something together when we get old enough?"

"What do you have in mind?"

"I'm a brass man. French horn."

"How many French horn duets do you know?"

"Oh, right ... Well ... Violin. There are lots of them."

"Yes, but it's a very hard instrument."

"Can't be as hard as what we're doing now."

"You're on! See ya at Roosevelt Hospital in March!"

They are into it now. Samuel, sways with the music, like a dancer. Gabe, erect, his mouth tight as he concentrates. Julia looks over at me and her eyes say, "It's going well."

I don't want to spook them, so I just stare forward and keep rooting. At some point, when they are halfway through, halfway home, and I realize they've got it, they are in sync, and they've got it, I relax and actually hear the music. And then, suddenly, it's over. And we cry.

I cannot tell you how many recitals, year after year after year, I have felt the tears come to my eyes. We've all felt it when our child has done something extraordinary. Hit a home run. Or recited a poem at school. Or brought home a surprisingly charming drawing, or reached out to hug an elderly friend with innocent compassion. But when you find yourself overcome with emotion because your flesh and blood is suddenly pushing beyond the bounds of your expectations, truly, truly surprising you at that instant with the command of something that is almost beyond your understanding, you become overwhelmed not with the simple pride that comes with "ownership," with being their parent, but, I think, with the awe that this child has invested himself in an endeavor beyond your control. He has become more than your baby. He has become a particular unique self that throws you. It literally throws you and causes your chest to fill and causes you to cry with a deep release that is a wonderful combination of pride and awe and love.

The recital audience applauds wildly. I don't frankly know how well they played. It sounded good to me. They got through it. And they were cute! We gave them big hugs and their teacher,

Katherine, a bouquet of flowers, and we all went out to a festive, neighborhood Italian restaurant, where we were so excited and relieved that Samuel left his violin behind. Gabe reminded him, after we'd picked it up the next day, "Remember when you were little and we met Wynton Marsalis in the elevator on our way up to a lesson with our old teacher? And Mommy was holding my violin? And he said, 'Boys, always carry your own instruments!'"

"Yes Gabe, I remember."

"Well?"

"I was eating pasta. We were celebrating. I had a sip of Dadoo's wine. I ... I ... I was drunk!"

We spring for a taxi to take us home, and on the way down to the village, packed in the cab, they both talk at once.

"It's terrible; when we're playing we can see the teachers all taking notes in the first row."

"I didn't see them Sam, I was into the music"

"I was 'into the music' too, but I still saw them!"

This banter reminded me of our summers in the Berkshires, when every Friday night we'd pile into the car with a picnic basket and blankets stuffed in the boys' old wagon in the back and head off to Tanglewood, The Tanglewood Music Festival, summer home of the Boston Symphony Orchestra, only ten minutes from our farm house. The boys would chirp in anticipation of the concert, "Emanuel Ax is playing the Mozart piano. He's the best."

"Maybe he'll play at the chamber concert."

"Yes, remember we saw him two years ago with Malcom Lowe playing the Beethoven Sonatas?"

"Can we sit in the balcony behind so we can watch his fingers?"

From their first visit to Tanglewood, the boys were entranced by the luscious rolling grounds. Green upon green on a summer evening. Views of the Berkshire Hills in the distance. Stockbridge Bowl, the sweet lake that glistened out beyond the Tanglewood trees. The grounds are dotted with small cabins, rehearsal rooms, where, strolling around, you can hear young musicians practicing. When we arrived, the boys would rush to Ozawa Hall, the small concert hall, and get box seats just off the stage, so they could be close and see the performers. Watch Anna Sophie Mutter's fingers as they danced up and down the neck of her violin. Or we'd sit up in back of the stage so we could watch Emanuel Ax's fingers as they danced along the keys of the piano.

And the best part—the concert was free. Included in the price of your "lawn ticket."

After the Chamber concert, we'd stroll to the lawn where we'd left our picnic unattended atop our old wagon. We'd spread out a blanket and eat our roast chicken as the evening sun descended and the first stars came out. We could hear the BSO warm up. A cue to the boys. The boys had become obsessed with the BSO and had started to dress like them. We'd found in a thrift shop boy-sized white dinner jackets, just like the ones the orchestra members wore. So they dressed up as BSO members, in the white jackets and dark pants and ties, and when the lights flashed that the concert was about to start, the well dressed boys simply walked into the Shed ... right past the ushers, too charmed by twin boys in BSO-like garb to stop them ... and ran down the aisle looking for empty seats. Julia and I lay on the lawn to listen. And would often be joined by the boys for the second half, so we could all snuggle together under the blankets, looking up at the stars, taking in the glorious music. Friday after Friday after Friday, all summer long we went. And summer after summer after summer. By the end of many of the concerts, Sam had fallen asleep under the blankets, and we'd have to pick him up, put him in our wagon, and roll him, fast asleep, across the lawn, down the hill, into the parking lot where we'd lift him, still sleeping, into the car.

As the boys grew, we had to find larger-sized white jackets. And soon they were vociferously analyzing each performance. Van Cliburn was too slow. Yo Yo Ma was showboating. Hillary Hahn was perfect. Better than Joshua Bell. Subtler. Week after week. Year after year. Composer after composer. Performer after performer, we could see their knowledge and enthusiasm growing before our eyes. I remember when the kids were about eight and we were in the car, driving to the country, and the radio announcer said, "Next, we will hear Gershwin's 'Rhapsody in

Blue.'". Sam shouted from the back seat. "Turn that off! No rap music!"

It is six months after the recital. A chilly November evening in New York. My sons are playing, one in the living room, one in his bedroom, preparing for another recital. Over and over and over they play their pieces. I am working in the kitchen on a rewrite of a play, having difficulty with its ending. I remember what the great playwriting teacher, John Gassner, once said, "If you're having trouble with the third act, rewrite the first." He's usually right. I flip back to act one, and start reading. It's so damned hard. Rewriting. But writing *is* rewriting. I think Aeschylus may have said that.

Gabe walks into the kitchen after practicing. "Boy, this is really hard." A lesson had come full circle. I had told them as little boys, "Always do something difficult. It will be more interesting while you do it and more rewarding having done it." And here was Gabe telling me how hard the violin is, but still pushing to be good at it—reminding me, reminding us, cautioning us, that when we are confronted with something difficult, we had to keep at it. After a day at school, and hours of homework, he and his brother would pick up their fiddles and still play for two hours, late into the night. So that now, when I am faced with a difficult rewrite or Julia with an impossible negotiation, or even some more mundane roadblock, we cannot "phone it in." We had to approach it with the vigor and integrity that we saw our son's giving to their violins. Whether my sons remembered my advice of years ago, they had lived it and were now *teaching us,* reminding us to live it ourselves.

And so, what I had learned from my children also, and maybe most of all, was that, if you teach them well, they will keep you honest.

SCENE: SAMUEL AND GABRIEL'S BEDROOM.

(Lee is there.)

> LEE

Guys, you really have to empty some of the stuff out of your backpacks. They weigh a ton. It's not good for your backs.

> SAM

We will.

> LEE

When? I asked you last week.

> GABE

Dadoo, we're busy.

> LEE

You're always busy. And it never gets done.

(He picks up Gabe's backpack)

Jesus! Do you have a cinder block in here?

SAM

I'm trying to write a paper.

LEE

Why not take five minutes? Five minutes and just triage the stuff you don't need every day.

(They ignore him)

Five minutes. What difference can five minutes make right now?

GABE

We'll do it, Dadoo. We'll really do it. But not now.

LEE

Okay. How about if, I do it. I pretty much know what you need and don't need.

(He picks out a huge book from Gabe's backpack)

Do you need this humongous math book every day?

                    GABE SAM

Yes! Dadoo!

(Dadoo exits, Julia passes in the hall)

                        JULIA

Everything okay in there?

                        LEE

Perfect.

CHAPTER TWENTY

DON'T TAKE IT PERSONALLY

One talent that is missing from my repertoire, which lacks an array of other talents including: repairing a car, folding laundry neatly, sustaining a diet, and reading a newspaper quietly in bed, is waking up my kids for school.

I *think* I am good at it. (I also think I'm good at speaking Italian, but my family hides from embarrassment when I try it. Having the guts to do something and having the talent should not be confused.) But what little skill I had at waking my kids was sorely tested when the boys started high school. The public high school was not walking distance from the apartment, so Sam and Gabe took the subway uptown (uptown!) to Fifty-Ninth Street and then walked (usually ran) two very long blocks west and two north to the school, wearing full, *very heavy* backpacks. And sometimes carrying their violins and/or fencing gear. School started at 8:00, so they had to leave the house at the latest at 7:30. While Julia walked the dog, it was my job to wake them. I'd walk into my kids' room at ten to seven and say, in the sweetest, happy-go-lucky tone, "Gentlemen, it's ten to seven. Time to get up. Chilly today. Wear lined pants. Long sleeve shirts. Up and at 'em. Adam and Eve!" And I'd turn and walk to the kitchen to start making breakfast. I'd put on water for tea. Get out cereal, juice, etc, and start making the boys' lunches. I'd check the clock. Seven. Time for a second call.

"Okay gentlemen, it's seven o'clock. You have one half hour to shower, if you so choose, and dress and eat and go. I suggest you get up. Now." Notice the happy-go-lucky has left. It's now down-to-business. But still civil.

I'd return to the kitchen and lovingly make ham and cheese sandwiches on rolls. New rolls. They didn't like the old rolls. The old rolls were too soft. These are hard rolls. They seem too hard. I toast them briefly to soften them. (Did my mother do this for me?) I'd check the clock. It's 7:10. I'd walk urgently into their room.

"Okay! It's 7:10. You have twenty minutes. Let's get to it. Sam, Gabe—get the hell up! This is your last call!"

Back to the kitchen. Where are the plastic containers for their lunches? Back to the bedroom. Open their backpacks. There they are.

"Guys, I've been asking you since second grade to bring your lunch boxes to the kitchen *after school.* Don't you think you could start doing that?"

Back to the kitchen. Happy-go-lucky and Down-to business have been replaced by Get-your-ass-in-gear! I pack their lunches. It's 7:15. Back to the bedroom.

"It's 7:15! You have fifteen minutes to dress, eat, and leave. Are you or are you not going to get up?"

Sam raises his head and in a deftly sardonic tone he says, "Dadoo, we heard you the first time."

They have been lying in bed for a half an hour. Comatose. The previous times, I came in to lovingly remind them of their obligation to get out bed. Now I am frothing and Sam can say to me in this God-what-I-have-to-put-up-with tone, "We heard you the first time." I wanted to shout, "If you heard me the first time why didn't you get up the first time?" And oops, I actually said it. "If you heard me the first time, etc. ... "

"We hear you every time. How can we *not* hear you?"

"Then why don't you *say* something, like 'Thank you, Dadoo. We'll be there shortly.'"

"Oh please!"

"Oh please, what? Last year I woke you up at 7:00 o' clock and you said that's wasn't enough time, so this year I get up at 6:30, so I could wake you at 6:45, and you lie there till 7:15. What's the point of waking you early if you lie in bed anyway?"

"We like to lie in bed."

"We like to just go back to sleep for five or ten minutes."

"It's a special pleasure."

"It's not a pleasure for *me* to come in here two and three times and get no response. It's not a pleasure to have you then, at 7:15, rush to get dressed and bolt down your breakfast and frantically stuff your backpacks and shout at us that you are missing your Spanish book or your calculator or your watch. It's exhausting. And not fun. Every morning, the same tense ritual!"

And then I said the wrong thing. "If you really cared about me, you'd get up the first time I asked, so we could have a relaxed morning"

Parry. Repost! "Oh puleeze. This isn't about *you*."

"Don't take it personally. Why do you take it personally? It's not your problem."

"If we're late, it's our problem."

"Why do you have to make it *your* problem?"

"Why do you have to take it personally?"

This wasn't fair. Now both of them at once were having the last word.

I was about to explode. Fortunately, Julia was back from walking the dog, and she interceded. She kicked me out of the boys' room, closed the door, and did as she always did—got them to get up and get dressed, using guile and charm and patience. All of which I flunked in Child Rearing 101.

I went to the breakfast table. Sat. Drank my tea and read the disheartening headlines in *The Times*. I wondered, what's so awful about saying, "If you really cared about me, you'd get up"? Julia came into the kitchen and I said it to her. She calmly replied, "What's wrong is, you make something fairly unimportant—*getting* to school on time—into how much they care about you. You blow your wad on a trivial issue."

"Hey, *they* care about being on time. When they're late they go ballistic. Why can't I care *for* them?"

"Because you *can't*. They're already on emotional overload. They have too much homework. Not enough time to practice violin and you bring *your* tension into their life, and they don't want it. They want calm."

"Calm doesn't work. I try calm the first time I wake them. They ignore me."

"They hear you."

"They ignore me. How do I know they hear me?"

"They tell you every morning that they hear you. Believe them."

"But they don't get up. And they always run late, and it makes breakfast pure chaos!"

"They know that. But when you act up, they can blame it all on you."

"Act up? I'm sorry. I only 'act up' because they lie there and say smart-ass things to me. They don't seem to care as much as I do."

"They care about being on time. They *don't care* that it drives you crazy."

"Why not? Why not?"

"They have too much on their plate to care about that."

"With all I do—with all we do for them, they don't care?"

"Don't go there. They are very, *very* appreciative kids. They know how much we do for them. They know how lucky they are. They just don't want it thrown in their face."

The boys came to the table. They ate one half a bowl of cereal, each. Sipped some tea. Late as they were, Gabe sneaked a look at *The Times*.

"Bush is acting as if he'd won a landslide."

Sam still half asleep adds, "Or stole a landslide."

Gabe finds the sports page. I check the clock. Bite my tongue. Julia to the rescue.

"Gabe, it's 7:35. Read the paper when you get home!"

And suddenly they were up and off.

"Your lunches!" I shouted.

Sam came back, grabbed the lunches. Turned.

"What's for lunch?"

"Ham and cheese on a roll."

"Again?"

I try to steel myself, the way I did when Gabe stood up in his crib and said, " No, I want mommy." I try *not* to take it personally.

The fact is, as a writer I am always trying not to take any form of criticism or rejection personally. Recently, I got a critique on something I had written that it was "boring." My first reaction was the same as when a young cousin of mine told me that Mozart was boring. I (un-tactfully) told her that it was boring because she didn't understand it. But, I was sure that this "critic" had fully understood my work. It just bored him. What does that mean—boring? It's completely subjective. One man's episode of *Survivor* is another man's symphony by Mozart. I have never written a boring thing in my life! Sometimes scenes drifted to the slightly bland. Sometimes dialogue tended toward the obvious. But I prided myself on the originality of my work, and especially the vibrancy of my characters. How could a vibrant character be boring? I could feel my stomach churning. I was angry. I was taking it personally. How could I not? I'm sure my mechanic takes it personally if, after he repairs my car, I tell him that it still doesn't run well. I'm always careful to say, "Y'know, I really wanna thank you for all the time you spent trying to get rid of that ear shattering engine noise, but … *it's still there.*" I still like him. But the noise is still there. At what point, when the noise isn't fixed, do I cease to like him? At what point when a studio executive tells me that my script just doesn't have enough edge do I want to tell him take his edge and shove it. The fault lies, Dear Brutus, in me. When I am finished with a script, I know it's not perfect, but think there's a chance that it is perfect. I am just waiting for that first response, "Perfect!" It never comes. Frankly, anything less than, "Perfect", I take personally. I'm sorry. I am what I write. I know I'm not supposed to be. But I am. I have often tried to distance myself from what I write. And when rehearsing a play, I can indeed look at what's taking place on stage and say, "This isn't working. This is … yes … boring." And I can fix it. As if I'm fixing some other writer's work. I have to be able to do that in order to function. To improve my work. But, that's a learned skill.

Like knowing just how much to lean left on skis to avoid hitting a tree. I taught myself to distance myself from my material so that I could work on it. I had to do this in order to make what I had written better. I had to fall out of love with my words and my investment in my work and just fix the damn noise in the engine. And yet ... on opening night, when the audience doesn't laugh at a moment that I was sure was the funniest thing I'd ever written, I am hurt. I take it very personally.

Someday I'll learn not to invest so much in waking up my kids. Meanwhile, I'm trying to learn from them, what I taught myself during the rehearsals of a play; just do your job. Make the play work as if it were written by a stranger. OK. So, I'm going to wake them up every morning and pretend I'm not their father. I'm just the wake up guy. Let them hurl abuse at me. I don't care. I'm cool.

Yeah. Right.

SCENE: THE LIVING ROOM OF THE
NEW YORK APARTMENT.

(Samuel and Gabriel burst in, home from a long day at high school. Lee and Julia are having a quiet late afternoon tea.)

SAM

(Thrusting a piece of paper at Julia)

Look at this. Look at our reading list. All the books were written in the last thirty years. There's no Dickens. No Thackeray. No Tolstoy.

GABE

Tolstoy? Are you kidding. There's no book over two hundred pages.

SAM

They think the kids can't read complicated language.

GABE

They think they're making the kids feel better by giving them stuff that's easy to read. That *relates* to their life.

SAM

But what they're really doing is patronizing them.

GABE

They want to make them feel smart by giving them something easy to read, but the message they're sending is, "You're not smart enough to read really great literature."

SAM

Essentially they're keeping students in their place. It's elitist!

GABE

It's awful.

SAM

What a system!!!

LEE

Anyone for tea?

CHAPTER TWENTY-ONE
TEACHERS

Teachers have it pretty good. At least with our children. They get the kind of respect we only dream of getting. I remember when my kids were in, I don't know, third grade, and I asked them when they got home, if they could please take their lunchboxes out of their backpacks and take them to the kitchen. They didn't do it. I reminded them. They didn't do it. Frustrated, I finally said, "If your teacher asked you to do it—you'd do it!" Well did I get flack about that! Everything from, "My teacher doesn't ask the way you ask" to the more nuanced and contemporary, "Oh please!"

My kids, rarely, if ever took their lunch boxes to the kitchen when they came home. It was a battle I was not going to win. Their minds were filled with too many issues of real importance for them to bother with such trivial matters as their lunch boxes. I gave up trying to lighten their backpacks. That they could avoid my current back problems by not running across town with twenty-pound loads on their backs was something they'd have to learn on their own. What the hell, I never did learn that if you put your shoes away before bed, you won't trip over them on your way to pee at two in the morning.

I didn't have to listen to them say, "Oh please" anymore. Did they ever say that to one of their teachers? Of course not. They hadn't grown up with one of their teachers. They hadn't seen their teacher sitting on the toilet reading *National Geographic* and brushing his teeth at the same time. They hadn't seen their teacher shout "You stupid jerk" to himself when he lost in the computer something he'd just written. They hadn't seen their teacher overcook a very expensive lamb chop and then angrily fling it into the sink. No, their teachers, as flawed as they might be, had never displayed their private humanity with all its warts, and therefore had managed *not* to be seen by my children as ... well ... family members whom they can treat with an easy lack of respect. After all, what are families for?

I know families where the children still address the father as "Sir." I actually have a secret over-the-top admiration for these fathers. How the hell do they get their kids to do that? I've always wanted to ask one father I know who gets the "Sir" response how he worked it. Did you ... I mean ... when Brad uttered his first word ... when he looked at you and pointed to the dog and said, "Doggy," Did you snap back, "Doggy, *Sir!*" Do you have to start that young? Or did you wait till they had a small vocabulary. When they said, "Dad, I want more ice cream." did you say, "No, Brad, it's 'May I have some more ice cream, Sir?'" And when they banged their spoons on the table yelling "Ice cream, ice cream, ice cream" did you then pull out a riding crop and whack them across the hands and say, "It's, 'May I have more ice cream, Sir?' until they responded correctly? Or were you really good at it? Subtle. Did you start showing them old British movies where kids called their father "Sir" all the time, so they were inculcated with the idea by example? Or, did you patiently, each and every time the word "Sir" was left off after a sentence addressing you, say to them, "What word did we forget, Brad?"

I really wanna know. In my next life, I want to have kids that address me as "Sir." At least I think I do. I mean, even if it's, "Get a life ... Sir," I'd be pleased.

Teachers, *teachers* have always gotten that non-familial respect. But, they haven't avoided criticism. When Samuel was in kindergarten, his teacher told all the children to sit on the floor with their legs crossed and their hands folded.

"Criss-cross apple sauce."

Sam's hand shot up. "Ms. Spector, I'm not comfortable that way."

Ms. Spector responded patiently, "Well, we sit this way at Carpenter School so we don't bother our neighbor."

Sam was not satisfied, "But, if I'm not comfortable and I *don't* bother my neighbor, isn't that more important than a way of sitting?"

It was just the beginning of a long career of Sam's anti-establishment behavior. And to tell you the truth, I'd rather have my son give one response like that over a million "Sirs." So, along with that respect for teachers came a healthy skepticism about the whole system.

The first *major* confrontation came in fourth grade. They had a math teacher who was, to say the least, eccentric. She intimidated all the students. Rash outbursts. Worse, she was a past master at the art of humiliation. When the boys reported some of the put-downs she foisted on kids who were not prepared, I was appalled. When the boys were told that papers they had written were too good to have been written by them—that they must have had help from their parents—and she was going to take points off their grade because of it—we stepped in. We asked the principle for a meeting with the teacher. And with the teacher, and our boys present, we confronted her about all these issues. The plagiarism charge and humiliating remarks she made to the students. She had no defense and was suitably chastised by the principle. The boys had been uneasy about our doing this. It embarrassed them that we would march into school like this, but when they saw the results, they were impressed. We were impressed. A community school had listened … and responded to the complaints of parents in the community. The thing is, she wasn't a bad teacher. She was a good teacher with bad habits. I guess I think of myself as a good father with bad habits. This incident ends sweetly, because at the end of the year, the eccentric teacher took her entire class to a Yankee game.

"You really want to go to a Yankee game with her?"

"Sure, why not? It's the Yankees."

In tenth grade, their history teacher presented a problem. He was a good teacher. He was more than a good teacher—he was inspiring. But he gave voluminous homework assignments that he never read! I said, "So, just write any nonsense. Write … blah, blah, blah on the paper. Write, 'Thomas Jefferson was too smart for his own good.' If he's not going to read it, call him on it!" No, they couldn't do that. They wanted to play by the rules. They were given an assignment, they wanted to do it properly. And they wanted him to read it properly. We asked for a meeting with the principal. We got it. And Julia and I and the principal and the Assistant Principal sat with the history teacher and registered our complaint. His reply was, in essence that, "It doesn't matter what the kids turn in. If they were studying slavery, for instance, one child could turn in a drawing of a slave ship, while another wrote a detailed paper on slavery. It was about *participating.*"

"But, we responded, why should our kids spend so much time writing a detailed paper, if you're not going to read it? They are writing it so they can get your assessment of it. They're proud of what they write. They want some acknowledgment from you."

It went on like this, and the assistant principle finally urged him not to give homework assignments that he wasn't going to look at. Finito. This meeting took place early in the term. By the end of term, by June, the boys were enthralled with this teacher. He was a kind of neo-socialist. He was giving them a view of American history that was so off the wall ... so against the placid taken-for-granted view of America as the beacon of freedom and democracy that it appealed to their revolutionary urges. One of their textbooks was Howard Zinn's, *History of the American People*—a suspicious, if not cynical, view of our nation's history if there ever was one. He, Mr. Turner, was teaching them to question authority! To question everything they read. To question the very foundation of our history. And they loved it. They were questioning my authority all the time. Now they were given permission to question it big time.

What had begun with an anxious meeting about a teacher who seemed out of touch with our children's concern for fairness ended with the adoration of a teacher who helped transformed their way of thinking.

And they were to have several teachers of such an inspiring nature. Their math teacher, Mr. Galinor, their Biology teacher Mr. Mckenna—teachers who, even after their year with them was finished, continued to be touchstones in their education, and even became friends.

The boys practiced an odd kind of respect for their own parents. They were not always polite to us, but they deeply respected who we were, how hard we worked, and what we believed. And though they were always polite to their teachers, more polite than they might have been to us, they only showed them *deep* respect when they earned it. It took me awhile to realize that. To realize their different standards of respect. They could be flip with us and deferential to their teachers, but when their teachers behaved badly, they had the guts to call them on it. Or if intimated, to allow us to intervene. What I learned was, that they had learned something more important than a "yes, sir" reply. That they could be polite *and* outraged at the same time. A much more effective method than the pure outrage that I was wont to express to a tardy waiter, "When we tell you we only have forty five minutes to eat, you can't bring the meal forty minutes later!"

In the boys last year of high school, they confronted their most daunting situation. Gabe's English teacher, whom I shall call Ms. X, gave them, and indeed all of us, a trial in the art of patience. We'd encountered her before. In the boy's freshman year, they auditioned for her production (she's a director) of *The Fantasticks*. The boys learned the music in preparation for their audition, and Sam felt he had a good shot at a part. He auditioned and came home excited. "I was the best singer. I've got a good shot." A few days later, they were told that *no one* who had not previously worked with Ms. X on a play, would get a part. They were offered understudy roles. Sam was livid! It was bait and switch. Why weren't they told this *before* they auditioned? Why weren't they told they had no chance of getting a role. It was particularly cruel.

Now, we were to meet her again, and this cruel streak was to surface again. One of Gabe's assignments was to write a ten minute play. This he did ... and it turned out to be quite charming. But when he got his first grading of it, he found, attached to the play was a "grading sheet," in which points where given for various aspects of the play. Thirty points were just given to "formatting"—that is anything from spelling to not following the format she had laid out, i.e., stage directions in italics and characters names center with colons after them. I told Gabe to use my playwriting computer program. No, he said, your program is not accurate. "Accurate? It's exactly accurate. It's based on the template for what professional playwrights use." No, Ms X didn't want the program used by most playwrights, she wanted *her* program. If not ... points off. When I met with her to question why so many grade points were focused on what seemed irrelevant aspects of playwriting she said, "I'm teaching the students discipline. I'm teaching them to follow instructions. This is not about playwriting. It's not a playwriting course. It's a discipline course." I said, You mean if Eugene O'Neill were to submit *Long Day's Journey* and he got the formatting wrong, you'd lower his grade?"

When I relayed this to the boys, Sam jumped up. "Discipline? That's not discipline! We're disciplined. We do our work, and we do it well, and we don't need to be prodded to do it. *That's* discipline. What she wants is blind obedience!"

And he was right. She made up arbitrary rules... . so that she could teach her students to follow rules ... just to see if they could follow rules. Even if their plays were brilliant, it mattered little. First they had to learn to obey her rules. That was the preeminent lesson. She was killing the creative drive in the spirit of Mussolini.

But Gabe knew how to keep his eye on the ball. It wasn't that difficult to follow her narrow orders. Requirements for spacing, spelling, page numbers, could all be fulfilled easily enough, time consuming though they may be, and in the process he could take the notes she did give about actual playwriting and make his play better. This he did. And his grade improved. More important, his play improved. Then, the night before he was to hand it in, he panicked.

"It's not exactly ten pages. It has to be ten pages."

I looked at the text. "So, it's 9 and three quarters".

"She'll take off ... it has to be exactly ten."

"You're kidding."

"No!"

I quickly looked over the play. "No problem ... just take some of your dialogue and break it up. The mother has these lines here ... and the daughter interrupts, But, Mom ... And then the Mom continues. Zap! It was exactly ten pages. We high-fived. We had beaten the system. Well, we had given in to the system. Well, no, really we had seen the system for what it was ... and gamed it ... for the greater the good: handing in a damned good play.

Gabe had shown unusual patience. More than I had. My instinct was to storm into her office and call her a fascist. I didn't. Thank goodness. I played Gabe's game, and simply saw her manipulative nature for what it was and saw its relative unimportance in the overall scheme of things. He would not have to deal with her again. And he had written a good play. He had learned that sometimes you have to put up with this petty shit from people who have skewed agendas. Pick your fights.

He lost a lot of sleep, scrupulously formatting his play. He could have spent it polishing the prose on his history paper. But, as far as he was concerned, it was only sleep. He'd sleep when the semester was over. And, after all, she was going to get Sam the next semester, and, as he remembered from kindergarten—"criss-cross apple sauce"—Samuel did not suffer fools gladly.

SCENE: BROOKS BROTHERS STORE IN NEW YORK.

(Lee, Sam, and Gabe are shopping for suits for the boys)

GABE

Here are some nice suits, Dadoo.

(Lee comes over, looks at the price tag)

LEE

Yes, yes, but they cost a thousand dollars.

GABE

A thousand dollars?

SAM

That's ridiculous!

GABE

The one's we saw at the discount store were two hundred dollars.

SAM

How can they cost five times as much?

LEE

Well, maybe these suits are made better. Better material.

GABE

I'll bet there's not that much difference.

SAM

I'll bet the material and the labor costs pretty much the same. Y'know the difference? Advertising! You pay for the name brand advertising. And the store's advertising. The guy who made the material—the guy who made the suit—doesn't make anything. It's not fair. Let's get outta here!!

(The boys walk off toward the escalator to leave. The salesman comes over to Lee, who is still standing there)

SALESMAN

May I help you?

LEE

No, I think Brooks Brothers is a little too steep for us. I think my boys want to shop at Marx Brothers ... Karl Marx Brothers!

CHAPTER TWENTY-TWO

SEX, LOVE AND MONEY

One of my greatest regrets is that the boys never got to know my parents—the penalty for marrying late. My father died thirteen years before the boys were born. The boys were two when my mother left us. Thank goodness she met Julia.

On first meeting, Julia got the big welcome-to-the-family hug that she admitted she'd rarely gotten growing up with her own family. As my mother would say, "Around here we hug and kiss when you take out the trash." So, this sweet, blue-eyed, freckle-faced girl who was half my age (at the time, she's catching up) was suddenly brought to the bosom of the quintessential Jewish mother. Well not quintessential. Jewishness was not her dominant feature. There was no old-country accent. There was no smell of brisket throughout her apartment. There was no burden-of-life tone to her voice. She was like a Noel Coward character who happened to be Jewish. Behind all the sassy lines was warmth. And Julia loved it. And it didn't hurt my cause.

The spirit of my mom's generosity, infused in me and released in Julia, came full circle with our sons. Though they didn't "know" my mother, they acted as if they did. And spookily enough, the same for my dad.

My father had struggled through the depression, and it informed everything he did. It did not make him ungenerous. Never. It just made him wary of spending money he might not have tomorrow. Thanks to him, I've become a sort of a squirrel. Saving money when I have it. Never using a credit card if I don't have the money in the bank to pay the bill. Always looking for a bargain. But always remembering to splurge when the occasion is right

I remember him teaching me how to balance a checkbook as if it were one the great rites of passage in the Western World. The key to stability and life-long happiness was a balanced checkbook! I also remember the "sex talk" we had when I was, I guess, fifteen or sixteen. He came into my room and sat uneasily on the chair by bed.

"We should talk about … you know … sex and things"

I shrugged, "Okay."

He looked at me, shifted in the chair. Sighed.

"So, is there anything you want to know?"

"Nope," I said quickly.

"Good," he said, and got up and left the room.

The balance-the-checkbook talk took considerably longer. Consequently, my financial life has been far more consistent than my sex life.

My dad was conservative in the old fashioned way—i.e. you don't talk about sex, and you save your money. He was a *principled* tightwad. If he was going to spend money, it was going to be on something good. Except, of course, when my Mom would ask him to pick up some Jack Daniels Bourbon and he would bring home "Old Hickory," or some other unknown brand. My mom would say, "I wanted Jack Daniels." "Oh," my dad would say, "Bourbon is bourbon. It's all the same!"

"It's all the same to you. You don't drink bourbon!"

On the other hand, if I needed a suit, he'd go to the best men's store in town. There was no point in buying crap. You buy something good—it lasts. He didn't know from bourbon. He knew from suits.

And so, when the time came that I would be conflicted about spending a good deal of money on a gift for my wife, the boys came to the rescue. I was walking the dog in New York awhile back, when I saw a striking dress in a store window. I thought, My God, Julia would look great in that dress. She has nothing like it. It has an empire cut and a striped soft fabric that dropped almost to the ground. When the hell would she wear it? We don't go anywhere! Well, if it's $200.00, I could see buying it to wear on special occasions.

I went in. The saleswoman gave me the price: $400. Well that was it. Thank you very much. She held the dress up in front of her. She was my wife's size.

"Could you … . put it on?"

She went to change. I thought, "I'm not paying $400.00 for a dress. I know uptown women pay thousands for a dress, but they're married to men who are running the world. One of Julia's favorite jackets cost $5.00 at a thrift shop in Connecticut. She was joyful after that purchase. I was already getting depressed at the thought that this dress might look terrific on an actual person. The saleswoman reentered. She looked stunning! Julia would look magnificent. Well, I'm not paying $400.00 for a dress!

"It's the last one," she said.

Ohhhh, the old "it's the last one" ploy.

"Will you get more in?"

"They don't make them anymore."

Ohhhh. "The old they don't make them anymore" ploy.

I took a deep breath. "Let me think about it. Could you hold the dress till tonight?"

"Sure."

I left the store. Good. Leaving is good. Once you leave the store, the charm of the actual object fades. It's always good, before you make an impulse buy to leave the scene of the crime, the impulse, and allow the impulse to subside. I was now a block away and could feel my love of the dress now being overtaken by the practicality of not spending $400.00. She'll wear it—what, once every five years? If that.

I got home. Yes, the memory of the gorgeous dress was fading. No, it wasn't. I imagined Julia in it on the opening night of one of my plays. Even if the play was a disaster, she'd look great. It was one of a kind. It made no sense. The boys came home from school.

"I just saw a fabulous dress for Mommy. For her birthday. But I can't afford it."

"How much is it?"

"Four hundred dollars."

"Wow!"

"What's it made of?"

"I don't know. It just looks great."

"Is that a lot for a dress?"

"Sam, it's a lot for us."

"Right."

"What do you think guys?"

"We have money in our savings accounts. From Grandmom, from our birthdays. Why don't we help you?"

"We could pay half."

"I'll pay for the upper half!"

"Dadoo!"

"You guys really want to do that?"

"Yes! Sure!"

The ghosts of my parents had taken over the bodies of my children. The principled tightwad and the effusive hugger had fused in their immediate and generous response.

Julia came home.

I imagined her in the dress.

Opening night. Ooohs and Aaaaahs.

"Where did you get that dress?"

"My hubby and my boys gave it to me for my birthday."

Ooooooh.

I called the store. Hold the dress. I'll pick it up tonight.

I did.

A week later, on her birthday, she tried it on. She looked incredible. The boys and I looked at each other and knew we'd done the right thing. I don't know what I would have done if they had not joined in the purchase. I was happy to have no regrets. I was happy she was pleased. And I was most happy that it had come from all of us. Me, my sons and my mom and dad.

SCENE: THE NEW YORK KITCHEN—DINNERTIME

JULIA

Do you guys know if you want to go to the same college or different colleges?

GABE

Maybe different colleges, but a half an hour apart.

JULIA

That's going to limit your choices.

GABE

Maybe the same college but we room apart.

JULIA

Big or small?

SAM	GABE
Big.	Small.

                    GABE

Mommy, the size doesn't matter. The quality of the education matters.

                    JULIA

Of course.

                    GABE

But we would like a beautiful campus.

                    SAM

Beautiful architecture.

                    GABE

Old. Gothic. Like Oxford.

                    SAM

With fireplaces in the room.

                    GABE

We want a nineteenth-century education.

LEE

Oh. Great. Will you be taking your manservant?

CHAPTER TWENTY THREE

THE GRAND (OR NOT SO GRAND) TOUR

In the boys' junior year of high school, we planned the requisite college tour. How many colleges could we hit during the ten-day spring vacation? How many fleas could dance on the head of pin? We didn't want to push it. See so many that they all blurred together. We decided to pick the farthest location, Chicago, fly there, rent a car, then drive our way back east stopping at colleges along the way. Piece o' cake. With a brief respite at the house in Massachusetts we scheduled eight schools. Piece o' cake. Had I forgotten how hard it is to eat cake?? I always take a bigger piece than I can eat. It's always too sweet. I always feel bloated and guilty after I eat it. Why don't I chose something healthier for me like ... a pear? Okay, with a little cheese on a cracker. Okay, with a few cookies. Okay, a dab of ice cream. And chocolate sauce. Stop! That's kind of what happened with the tour. It turned into a one-a-day marathon. What I found out was: (a) All college tours are alike. Some bright enthusiastic kid walks backward while you shuffle after him among ten other families as he/she points out *not* how good the education is at his/her college, but how good the food is! College is all about food. At Cornell (not on this tour) a young lady actually said, "Y'know ... we have so many courses here. I mean, like freshman year ... if you're an English major and like you don't wanna take a heavy duty lit course, you can take a course in the Simpsons!" We could have stopped the tour there. My kids were appalled. Sam jumped in, "It doesn't make sense. Cornell's a good school. Why do they think telling prospective students that they don't have to take rigorous courses is attractive?" Gabe followed, "Maybe the tour guides do it on their own. They think it's cool."

"They should be fired!! The girl spent ten minutes telling us about how someone got up on the roof of the dorm at Halloween and smashed pumpkins down on everyone. What's that?"

Julia calmly added, "You know you're allowed to have some mindless fun in college. Even a good college."

But, I couldn't help thinking. Cornell is a fine school. Several of my most interesting friends went there, so why in hell *would* the tour guide emphasize its silliest course. On the drive back, we made up a whole curriculum of silly college courses, including: "Wars and Whores: The Influence of Prostitution on Major World Conflicts," "Short !: Great Undersized Rulers from Napoleon to LaGuardia," "Farting and Parting: The relationship between Flatulence and Divorce in the Twentieth Century," "Losers: the Psychological Study of Great Losers in History from Caligula to Custer."

I wondered though, if there might be no place in the real world for my kids. They hated pop culture. The music. The TV. The movies. Did I need to find a time machine to launch them back at least fifty years? Was their childhood spent listening to Cole Porter songs and old musicals and watching movies like *Some Like It Hot* and, of course, the whole classical repertoire going to isolate them from most of the other students? It didn't seem to bother them in high school. They were in a rock band. Well, kind of a rock band. Guitar, drums, vocal, and two violins. But the selections were eclectic ... from Beatles to Blue Skies. They got on. Why was I worried? It didn't worry them. They were secure in the value of what they liked. I was an all too typical parent, worrying if *they'd* be liked.

On the current trip we planned to visit the University of Chicago then drive east to Ohio for Oberlin, Kenyon—more east to Philly for Swarthmore and Haverford. A weekend break, then a flurry of Trinity, Wesleyan, and Yale, if we could squeeze it.

They all did run together, but more often than not, I realized that in ten minutes I knew if I liked a place or not. Julia and the boys, intent on soaking up as much info as possible, did the tours. Chicago and Oberlin got to us right away. Chicago with it's neo-gothic splendor and it's rep for hard-core learning and Oberlin for its bucolic, laid-back, turn-of-the-century, small-town coziness. Forget the tours, sign me up at either one and let's go home. But we plodded on. The boys felt they had to see 'em all to really know what they wanted or didn't want. Kind of like dating. You find a knockout on your first date. No way are you going to say to him/her, "You're it. I know it. Let's cut the crap and get married and live happily ever after."

The best part of the trip, for me at least, was the delightful bed and breakfasts we stayed at—some on campus at Kenyon and Trinity. What the hell I thought, I'd had dreams of going back to college, but what I really wanted was to live at a bed and breakfast on a beautiful campus and kind of be back at school, except I wouldn't have to go to classes and my room would be a lovely suite overlooking green lawns and stately buildings. (Actually many schools have picked up on my fantasy and now have retirement villages on or near campus for just such romantics as me.) At my old alma mater, Trinity, we were able to delight in a dinner with some of my old profs and in the memories evoked walking the long walk on the exquisite campus. But my evoked memories had no influence on the boys. They wanted a really old-fashioned, challenging school, with fabulous rustic old buildings. What they really wanted was Oxford.

In the fall, at Rosh Hashanah, when high school was closed for the Jewish holiday, we of course celebrated the new year by visiting Yale. (Doesn't everybody?) Yale seemed to perk their interest. Gabe was particularly taken with the architecture, the old-world feeling of the campus. Sam pressed the guide for specifics about the curriculum and seemed pleased with the responses. Julia and I liked the idea that the school was only an hour and a half from New York and the Berkshires. "That's not a consideration," Gabe quipped. We couldn't say outright that we would like them close to home, but the fact is they had never ever been away from us for longer than ten days. And that was only twice! It was Julia and I who were anxious about the separation. The thought seemed not to bother them at all. Except of course, they mostly talked about going to the same school. They would have each other. We didn't *have* to be close by.

"What's the point of going away to college if you can see your parents every weekend?"

"Just because we're close, doesn't mean we want to see you."

"I know."

"We know, but what about the idea that *we* might miss *you*. And want to be able to see you without having to fly somewhere."

Gabe straightened up. "That's not a consideration. We're going to the best college for us, not the best college for you."

"Oh, Gabey. You're so tough," I replied.

Julia to the rescue. "Gabe, Dadoo's just trying to tell you that we'll miss you."

"I know. I know. And we'll miss you too. But … "

I walked away. Gabe ran up after me. "Dadoo, we'll miss you too. But distance is not the prime consideration. The quality of the college is."

"Gabey, I *know* that."

"Yes ... yes. Okay. Okay."

An awkward silence. As your kids get older, everything has another meaning. Every little disagreement is not only about the subject of the disagreement, but about his declaration of independence. I took his hand, and we walked on through the campus quad.

Touring Yale brought up old memories. I had gone to a year of graduate school at the Drama School, but, in fact, I never saw most of the campus. I just walked from my apartment the two blocks to the drama school. I saw little else. Seeing the whole campus for the first time, it was impressive. Who knew? The schools get you by their campuses. You imagine, *I could live here*. And then a year later they tell you in your rejection letter, "No, you can't." But, even though their grades were good, we were realistic about the limited possibilities of the elite Ivy schools. And in some ways, I think the boys resisted those schools, simply because of an admirable resistance to their very eliteness. Harvard was of course, Harvard... but so what? It was the flip side of Groucho Marx's famous, "I don't want to belong to any club that would have me as a member." They were saying: these places, the Yales, the Harvards, the Princetons, have the air of being so exclusive that it turns us off. Was it self serving? "If they're going to reject me I don't want *them*." Or was it an honest reaction to this air of exclusivity?

But then again, they did apply to Oxford. There was "exclusive" and there was "Old World steeped-in-history exclusive."

But, Oxford rejected them.

And so they were accepted at the two schools they liked, Oberlin (with its Music Conservatory) and ... the University of

Chicago ... with its scary, albeit cryptically funny motto: "Where Fun Goes To Die."

So the following spring, after acceptance, we went back to see those two schools to make THE CHOICE.

When you revisit a school after acceptance you generally go on a designated "look-see" weekend. Hundreds of other kids and their families descend on the campuses. Big receptions. Lectures. Not like the first visit "Rah-Rah-Why-Our-School-Is-Terrific" type stuff. Some very helpful Q's and A's about fields of studies. We wanted to know of course just how our little violinists would find a place in the music department. And how it compared to a place like Oberlin, which, after all, did have its own conservatory. But again, the major thing is zeitgeist. What does it feel like being there? And now, actually sitting in a class, there—could Gabe or Sam imagine themselves being here?

It's something I never did. Nor my wife. Both of us picked a school after a fast tour, and then, when we got accepted, we went. My interview at Trinity was on a gray, gray day with a gray, gray admissions officer—so boring I had to ask him questions so he could stay interested in me. But I ended up going there. And I ended up loving it. So much for the thoroughness of our mission. The boys decided they'd go to a sampling of classes in subjects they intended to take. Philosophy. Calculus. Music theory. They also stayed overnight with some students in a dorm to get a feel for the students. We stayed overnight at the International House to get a feel for sleeping in a small room on a narrow bed. The next day we asked them about their dorm stay.

"It was okay. The kids were slobs. Dirty clothes all over the place."

"You mean like your room at home?"

"Oh much worse!"

They hadn't really had time to talk to the kids in the dorm, pick their brains. It was a bit frustrating. But Sam found some solace in one late night foray.

"Some kid was playing piano in the lounge and I jammed with him and that was fun!"

The boys had mixed feelings about Chicago. They loved the campus. The noble goal of the school, which touted itself as "The Life of The Mind." But they were disappointed in some of the kids they met and were appalled that several students surfed the net on their computers during class. But the place did intrigue them.

"The philosophy prof was great."

"He did a lecture on Hegel. Really impressive."

"Calculus was over my head, so ... I don't know."

"And if it was over Sam's head," Gabe added, "You can imagine what it was for me."

The University of Chicago is set in the village of Hyde Park, within the city of Chicago, and the ambience of its neighborhood streets and houses and the majesty of its gothic buildings isolates it from the roar of a big city a half hour up the drive on Lake Michigan. It gave the college an availability. A warmth.

That morning we packed ourselves into the car and headed southeast to Ohio. Driving into Oberlin is like driving into the past. The village green that greets you, surrounded by Italianate college buildings and main-street stores, feels like you are back in 1890. Horses and carriages should be clomping their way down those streets. Women in long skirts, holding parasols, should be walking the green, arm and arm with men in long black hats and topcoats. You are immediately calmed.

We dropped in for dinner at a school hangout, a Mexican place. Well, OK, they didn't have Mexican restaurants in 1905, but what this place did have was good food and a young music student sitting in the window playing Scarlatti on the harpsichord. We bought him a margarita for fortitude. And after dinner we walked to the conservatory to see if we could luck into a recital. A young Korean violinist happened to be doing one and we sat in. Exquisite. A wonderful dessert. But yet ... maybe, just maybe the ice cream store would be open for more. Cones in hand we paraded down past the Mexican restaurant. There in the window, still playing Scarlatti was the student harpsichordist. We went back to our room at the Inn and the boys went off to the conservatory practice rooms with their violins—to practice.

They didn't take their violins on the trip just because they were going to be staying at Oberlin, with its music conservatory, they took them whenever and wherever we went. Even on all our trips abroad. As Gabriel told me often, "If you don't practice every day, there's no point in playing."

Most times, to save money, we were all booked in the same hotel room, and the boys practiced as there as best they could—usually one in the bathroom and one in the bedroom—while Julia and I tried to read or nap to the din of the repeated exercises. Once, on a trip to Amalfi, while Gabe played in the tiny bathroom, Sam practiced out on the balcony, serenading a local fishmonger, cleaning his catch. On the rare occasion we stayed at a large hotel, like the Holiday Inn in Philly for my high school reunion, Julia phoned the desk and asked if there was an empty conference room the boys could practice in. I think on our first trip to Chicago they commandeered the empty ball room. "Great sound, Mommy. Come listen!!"

At Oberlin, at midnight, the boys returned to the room after practicing in the conservatory practice rooms.

"Mommy, Dadoo, we came back past the Mexican restaurant and ... "

"The student was still in the window playing Scarlatti."

"He's been playing for five hours!"

"Nonstop!"

"Nonstop? That's not easy on Mexican food."

"Booo!"

Fun may die at Chicago, but music never does at Oberlin. The next day the boys were due to meet a student guide and stay overnight at a dorm room and then visit classes. I was alone with the boys after driving Julia to the airport to fly back New York for work. We nosed around the campus and returned to the room. And while I lay down for a nap, the boys hit my computer. They were surfing the college curriculum for classes they wanted to take the next day after their dorm sleepover.

As I lay on the bed, half awake, I could hear them talking about the classes. They wanted to take the same ones they'd taken at Chicago in order to make a ready comparison. Cognizant of their sleeping Dad, they spoke quietly as they huddled over the computer, deciding which classes to take. Lying there, I was wafted back to when they were tots—when I would do morning duty and take them down to the piano room at crack of dawn, and set them off playing "restaurant" while I dozed on the day bed. I would listen to them making the food, talking in their limited vocabulary about how to make the scrambled eggs I ordered. I heard them discuss what an English muffin was. What to serve the tea in. Nothing made me happier than napping there while they played and chatted. And here I was, fifteen-plus years later, napping while they chatted about what classes to observe. Feeling the same comfortable bliss I had felt before.

The boys were focused. Dogged in their task of picking out the right classes to attend, much as they had been in finding just the right breakfast to serve Dadoo years before. Had they been taught this ability to focus? Did it happen because they were twins and they always had to bargain with each other and find solutions as a team, and therefore were forced to do things more thoroughly? Whatever the reason, as I listened to them carefully choose their classes, they showed me that every decision merits focus. Sure, you can go too far. How many times had we been late because the boys couldn't decide what attire would be best for a particular occasion. My "just put something on" was always met with derision. The implication: you can't be careful in your choices just some of the time!

The intervening month and a half was fraught with discussions about which of the colleges they wanted to attend. They re-read the catalogues. We had an old friend, an Oberlin alumni and booster, over for dinner and they peppered him with questions. They called my cousin in Philly, who had graduated from Chicago twenty years before, and grilled him. They could not get enough information, and the more they got the more conflicted they became.

"Just put both names on the dart board and throw a dart," I joked.

They were not amused.

May 30! The deadline. The night before they *had* to decide, the boys, with doubts about Chicago engendered by their disappointment about some of the students, decided to call the Dean of Admissions and "confront" him with their doubts. I left them alone in my study to make the call. They wanted me nowhere in sight. But, as it turned out, nature called just as they placed the call and I was next door in the bathroom as they connected with Dean O'Neill and spoke to him on the speakerphone. So, I heard it all. It was impressive. Gabe, like a district attorney put it right to the dean. They loved the school, but were disappointed in the lack of intellectual fervor of the students.

"Your college brochure advertises the college—right on the cover—as "The Life of The Mind."

Dean O'Neill paused and then, just easily, simply, told them that certainly they would meet some students who did not live up to that standard, but that by and large they would find that that standard was a template for most of the student body, and if they gave the school a chance they would find what they were looking for. He was impressive. And when the boys hung up and I entered the room as if I had heard nothing, they admitted as much. They were still not completely decided. And the next morning, deadline day, they sat with their mother and me and as they talked we both realized that, though they loved both schools, they really wanted to go to Chicago because its reputation as the "smart school" would be a badge of . . .well, "smartness." As boys who wanted an old fashioned hard-core education, it would set them apart in a way they always wanted to be set apart. It would make people think, when they told them "We go to the University of Chicago," that they must be smart. That they must love learning. It was the badge they wanted to wear.

Too often we're too shy to admit that we want a make a choice that boasts for us. We don't want to actually boast. That's too crude. Too egotistical. But we want to let others know something about us that makes us proud.

It's not done lightly. It's done by many choices. They want to dress up for the theater. They want to wear a jacket and a vest and tie and nice shoes to say to anyone and everyone, "This is an occasion for us. This is something we love. And we're dressing up to honor it." Being proud of their intelligence, they chose a school that was a wardrobe that reflected who they were.

SCENE: LIVING ROOM, NEW YORK APARTMENT.

(The boys burst in the door)

SAM

Our band is playing for graduation!

GABE

We play some of our set songs before all the speeches, and then, when the class marches up to get their diplomas...

SAM

We play "Pomp and Circumstance."

JULIA

You play "Pomp and Circumstance" with two violins, drums, base, keyboard and an electric guitar?

SAM

Yes!

LEE

No vocalist?

GABE

"Pomp and Circumstance" has no lyrics.

LEE

How about this? (he sings to the tune of Pomp and Circumstance)

We're finishing High School

It wasn't a nice school.

SAM

Dadoo, cool it.

CHAPTER TWENTY-FOUR

RENAISSANCE

The summer after the boys graduated from high school, the summer before they were due to leave for college, we decided to celebrate their rite of passage (and my birthday) with a trip to our home away from homes—Roma!

They graduated on a sunny morning in June, and only hours later, we were aboard a plane, taking off for London. Why London? Our old friend, the actor Tim Piggot-Smith, was starring in *Pygmalion* at the Old Vic. We hadn't seen him onstage since he'd appeared in New York with Kevin Spacey in O'Neill's *The Iceman Cometh*. We'd primed the boys with episodes of his Masterpiece Theatre series, *The Jewel and The Crown* and G.B. Shaw was the family's favorite playwright. We stayed with our old friends in Peckham and drank up London: Tim's delightful Henry Higgins, followed the next day by Shaw's *Arms and the Man* at the National. Then Shaw-satiated, we took the Chunnel Train to Paris.

Why Paris? Because it's Paris, and because another old friend, Phillipe, was there, visiting his family from his home in Vietnam. Phillipe was a charming renaissance man. He'd flown Corsairs for the French in *their* Vietnamese War, had been a campaign adviser for President Giscard d'Estaing, then been a wine importer in New York, where he met, married, and divorced an old girlfriend of mine, *then* moved back to Vietnam, married a local girl and had son, Alexander, to add to his already large family. He has a Marc Chagall-like elfin charm. He's the resident conservative among our liberal friends, and, more than anything, he loves a good time. His pragmatic political views sometimes stunned (and delighted) the boys.

"Terrorism is an overrated threat. How many people have died at the hands of terrorists? Thousands. How many died in World War One? Millions. In Russia alone, in World War II twenty million people died. Considering all the violence in the history of the world, this is nothing to get excited about."

We dined and drank and drank and drank with Phillipe and his Parisian family, and the next afternoon were squired to see his nephew's string quartet play under the beauty of the magnificent rose windows in the church of Saint Chapelle. Requisite stops at the Musee' D'orsay, the Tuillieries and the little blue crêperie down the tiny street near our small, cozy hotel. As rain fell for the first time in the trip, we rushed to the train to catch the plane to fly over the alps to Rome.

Francesco's ebullient smile greeted us at the out of the way airport where we landed, and we crammed our luggage into his small car and careened off to Rome. We were subletting a wonderfully eccentric apartment in an area called "I Monti" which was on a hill overlooking the Forum. We indulged in all our Roman pleasures, eating, talking with our friends, eating, walking and ... eating. Then we left for a trip south, in a very "hot" rented Alpha Romeo, to meet a friend I'd first encountered on our trip in 1997, Letizia!

We'd met eleven years before. On a warm September afternoon, I entered the convent where I was teaching and started through the small cloisters to drink my coffee at a table in the quiet area in the back. A young woman was just entering from the nun's quarters as I passed. I think I literally stopped and stared. I know I smiled. And maybe nodded. And maybe even said, "Buon giorno." Did as many things as would keep me looking at her as long as I possibly could. She was exquisite looking. She smiled back. Replied, "Buon giorno."

"Sono Letizia."

"Letizia?"

"Si. You are with the college, yes?"

"Yes, I'm a professor. I'm teaching playwriting."

"Italian playwriting?"

"No. Just ... playwriting. In English. I'm American."

"I don't ... I am not seeing many plays. But when I do see them, I love to go. Do you know Pirandello?"

"Yes."

"I love Pirandello."

"Yes, he's ... wonderful."

"Do you write like Pirandello?"

"No. Nobody writes like Pirandello. That's why he's Pirandello."

She told me she was studying to be a nurse and working at the college for room and board. I asked her, "How long do you have to study to be a nurse?"

"Two more years."

"It's a wonderful thing to be. I ... I'm a writer. It's fun to write, but I can't say that I do much for the world."

"Oh yes. Writers are very important. More important than nurses."

"I don't think so. When I'm in the hospital, I want a nurse, not a writer."

Samuel and Gabriel had always admired how easily I met new people. Went up to strangers and struck up a conversation. It was especially easy in Italy. Hanging out in cafés. Italians love to talk and are all patient and indulgent with your awkward

Italian. Julia had met a couple from San Francisco, Alan and Diane, who had moved to Rome, and Julia ended up running with Alan and later, "repping" him as a writer. Our sons became friendly with theirs. But our ease with strangers did not rub off on the boys.

The following year, in October of '98, Letizia came to stay with us in New York for three months. I got her some volunteer work at St. Luke's Hospital. Then enrolled her in an English language course. She came home every night with her vocabulary list filled with useful idiomatic expressions so she'd sound really American. One problem. The expressions were from the 1940s.

"What means "bit the dust?"

"Oh, that's bite the dust. That's an expression that means 'to die.' But no one uses that anymore. It's from old detective movies, "He bit the dust."

"Si. Si … What means, "You are the 'cat's meow'?"

What time warp did her text book come from? When she arrived, the Yanks were in the world series, and the boys immediately took to her. Taught her baseball. Soon she had her favorite player. "Je-ter. Go Je-ter!" The boys, *embraced* her, and she became part of the family. They got her to join them trick or treating at Halloween, dressed up in a nurses outfit with long fangs as "Monster Nurse." And reveled in introducing her to an over-the-top American Christmas. Her infectiousness had opened them up to the joys of diving into a new friendship. And they gave back in spades. So that, ten years later, when we took a trip to southern Italy, to Taranto, to the small town of Pulsano to meet her family, we were part of a dramatic incident.

We met Letizia and her new husband, Paolo, and drove down to Pulsano from Bari. Pulsano is a small town in the Puglia area of the Italian boot. No one there would speak English. This was a challenge for the boys, who prepared themselves on the drive by studying an Italian textbook and barraging us with questions about how to say this or that. On the trip from Bari to her childhood home, Letizia told me about her family, especially her father, who was a builder but had, as young man, wanted to be a musician. A clarinetist. And he was good. But *his* father did not want him to be a musician, and so her dad put down the clarinet, *fifty years ago*, and had not played it since. We were welcomed at her family's house and feted with an endless home-cooked Italian meal, including home-made wine. (Strong!) And after the meal, Sam took out his violin and started riffing. Letizia's brother-in-law took out his guitar and joined him. We watched as they merrily floated from song to song when suddenly Letizia's father burst into the room—*playing his clarinet!* He joined in with them. He played with them. He was playing for the first time in fifty years. We laughed. We cried.

Sam and Gabe had learned from us the joys of meeting strangers and making them into friends, and now, thrown into a household of strangers, they were not afraid to jump in and try their rudimentary Italian to communicate with all of Letizia's family. And because of Sam's impulsiveness, jumping in and playing with these strangers, he had lured Letizia's dad out of his fifty-year funk and back to the joyous pleasure he had abandoned when he was a boy.

The boys were going to leave us in the fall. Off to Chicago—to a world of strangers. Would they carry this Italian spirit with them and embrace the new place and the new people? Could they improvise, even without their fiddles, and find another home away from home?

We would soon find out.

SCENE: THE BEDROOM OF THE
NEW YORK APARTMENT.

(Lee and Julia are getting ready for bed)

JULIA

I'm worried about you.

LEE

Oh?

JULIA

I think you're going to miss the boys more than I will.

LEE

That's possible.

JULIA

I think you're going to be a basket case.

LEE

You could be right.

JULIA

I hope you'll be okay, because ... because

(she is suddenly choking up)

I'm really, really, *really*, going to miss them.

(She bursts into tears. Huge sobs. Lee puts his arms around her and holds her as Sam enters the bedroom)

SAM

Is mommy okay?

LEE

She's fine. She's just worried about me.

CHAPTER TWENTY FIVE

SEPARATION AGREEMENT

You hear a lot about "the empty nest." How your kids leaving home either devastates you or, surprisingly, has little effect. Or becomes a blessing of silence and self-indulgence.

After our boys left for college in September, we were in the toilet. It was too quiet. What could we indulge ourselves in if we were used to doing everything with our kids? Dare we do something … just together? Didn't we do that before they arrived? Didn't we have fun without them? Sure. So … what's the problem?

We were hoist with our own petard. We had schooled our children, particularly around the dinner table, in the art of merciless self-expression. Tell us what you think. I admit that this would get out of hand a lot. We interrupted each other at will in an effort to express our opinions. I had grown up with vocal relatives to such an extent that, when at a holiday dinner, everyone was talking at once, my mother would shout out her inimitable "Take a number"! And if I dared to remonstrate with one of the boys for interrupting me, I would be countered with, "Well you do it all the time!" Trumped. It's tough to countermand a bad example you set for your kids. Even with such lame lines as, "The fact that it annoys you when I do it should teach you that you shouldn't do it!" Right.

You get the picture. Dinners, trips in the car, anywhere where we were bunched together and talking was the activity of the moment, the air was charged. It was often thrilling. Often exhausting. Fights broke out. The dog ran for cover. I stormed away from the table. Julia left to play the piano for solace. The boys often took a moralistic stand about things. Hurling invectives at us if we didn't respond correctly. There were times it seemed that they had the morals of Christ and the mouth of Lenny Bruce. But every night, every night we gathered for dinner. We lit candles. We had a real meal. We all liked to cook. I cooked more often than not, but Julia is a much more imaginative cook. I tended to fall back on old standbys.

"Oregano chicken again?"

Whoever cooked was intimidated because everyone was a bloody expert on food! Once, I was making dinner and Samuel wandered into the kitchen and came up to me at the stove and asked, "What are we having for dinner?"

"Scallops," I replied.

He nodded and said, "And what are you *doing* with them?"

Tough act. Food. Talk. Tough act. You'd think we'd look forward to their departure, so we could give our brains and our emotions a rest. We kind of did. But kind of, really, truly, didn't.

We drove a rented van crammed with stuff to the Chicago. We had been forewarned by a friend whose daughter had attended Chicago, that the separation ceremony would be tearjerker. We immersed ourselves in the details of moving the boys into their new dorm … a funky old hotel overlooking the lake. We helped them unpack and put up with repeated, "Mom, Dadoo, we can do that ourselves." We just wanted to keep busy before we would have to leave them. Finally, the scheduled welcoming ceremony at the soaring Rockefeller Chapel. A large banner hung across the front. "Class of '12" Class of '12? I remembered when I used to work at my college reunion weekends and the class of '12—1912—would parade by with a dozen old geezers holding up placards and wearing straw hats. I was older *now* than they were *then*. And my sons would graduate a hundred years after them. Life moved much too quickly. We sat, restlessly, looking at the makeup of other students. A dark, beautiful girl sat next to me. "Where are you from?"

"India. Mumbai."

"Why have you come all the way to Chicago?"

"I had to decide between Princeton and the University of Chicago, and I just thought the education here would be more rigorous."

Her friend, her new friend from Indonesia nodded in agreement. We listened to the welcoming speeches. History-of-the-college speeches. All delaying the inevitable, and finally the organ blared at the ceremony's end, and we all walked out of the

chapel and down the long walk to the college gate. At the gate a band of bagpipers played. Bagpipes thrill me and make me cry whenever I hear them. I had them accompany me and my best man to the altar at my wedding. This wasn't fair! The school was not making it easy for Julia and me to remain stoic. The boys kissed us both, Julia burst into tears, and the boys turned and walked to the college gate. Then, they stopped and turned back and waved to us, and I joined my wife and bawled. Upper classmen at the ready rushed up to us with boxes of Kleenex.

Well that would be the worst of it. The leaving is always the worst. It would be easy riding from here.

We flew home and started having meals alone. Together. It might as well have been alone. It was too damned quiet. And we couldn't call them. We'd given the boys cell phones against their will. Strident luddites and ardent nonconformists, they didn't want to be one of those kids who was glued to his cell phone.

"You know, when we go away to school, we're not going to call you every day on the cell phone like Melanie does to her mom."

"We don't even want the cell phones!"

"We'll write to you. Letters. Longhand. What's the point of going away, if you're going to babble on the phone everyday?"

"You could e-mail us," Julia interjected.

"Letters!" Sam insisted, "Like Henry James. Didn't you write letters, Dadoo?"

"Yes. Of course. With a quill pen."

They were getting a nineteenth-century education. They were damned well going to communicate in the spirit of that late, great era.

Because I was used to working alone in the apartment, writing there, being alone there most of the day, the boys absence didn't hit that hard. Only at dinner, when the hyped-up conversation about what was going on in the world was missing, did it seem off. But Julia felt it strongly. The vacuum. Her boys were gone. My boys were gone too. But *her* boys were gone. I think back to my experience being rejected by the boys in their cribs when I came to them and they said "I want mommy." Mommies have a special hold. Daddies can love their kids, but they were physically attached to Mommy for nine months. They came from mommy, and daddies simply cannot replace that relationship. It's Okay. Except when it's not. But no, it really is Okay. I felt that way about my mom. And I'm overjoyed that my boys feel the same way about theirs.

The downside of course is that Mommy hurts more when they leave. Or at least hurts longer. At least this Mommy. We wrote. On paper and by snail mail. And they wrote. Long, sometimes indecipherable, letters. But full of wonderful insights about this new experience. Not just college, but being away from home for the first time. For this long a time. This was a big deal. And Samuel, who was much more open emotionally, open in his letters, admitted that it was odd. It was difficult, but he knew it was important to have the experience. He reveled in the view from his room of lake Michigan and the spires of Chicago beyond. His honors calculus class was hard. Really hard. Even for him. But he liked the challenge. Gabe's accelerated Latin class left him breathless as he tried playing catch-up with all the other kids in class, who'd had several years of Latin in private schools. But he loved it. And both had auditioned for the school orchestra and gotten in. First violin. Good news. Bad news? They hadn't really had enough sight-reading training and were suddenly playing stuff that was way over their heads.

"What do you do if you can't play something?"

"We just keep moving the bow in time with the rhythm and hit the notes we can."

"You fake it?"

"Yeah. But ... we aren't alone."

"Why did they let you in the orchestra?"

"Our tone is really good. It impressed her. I had trouble with the fast passages, but she (the conductor) said, 'It's okay. You can learn those.'"

They had checkbooks, and cell phones, and debit cards—all things they'd never used before. We had sheltered them from the real world, and now they were faking it in the first violin section of the University of Chicago orchestra.

On-the-job training. The best!

And nothing prepares you for the empty nest thing. It's also on-the-job training. And little by little you get used to the perks. Now, neither of my kids comes into the room while I'm watching CNN or MSNBC and says, "What are you watching that crap for? You read *The Times*. What more do you need?"

No one comes into the living room as I'm about to watch the last few innings of a Yankee game and says, "I've got to practice."

"Can't you practice in your room?"

"Come on dad, it's just a Yankee Game."

"We have other rooms beside this one. This is the only one I can watch the ball game in."

"This is the best room to play in. It's ... you know ... It's nicer to play in a big room."

"But the game is only on in this room."

"You watch too many games."

"I rarely watch a game. This is a good. It's a pitchers' duel."

I get a look as he pulls out his violin. I give in. I go in the kitchen and turn on the radio and call up the sweet rationalization that has always comforted me. I really do prefer listening to games on the radio. Like I did when I was a kid. It has a warm, sentimental feeling for me. Ballgames on the radio.

Right.

These days, I find myself rationalizing less about little things and more about big ones. I tell myself that having the boys away is a learning experience. I mean for me. I spent a helluva long time avoiding marriage and family. I had reveled in being alone. But my life with my family has been the happiest years of my life and to see the sunny side of being alone again was difficult. But maybe this was my ultimate learning experience. I had learned more from my kids I think than they ever learned from me. I remember my father telling me a story when I sought his advice when I was on the verge of getting married the first time. I was at sixes and sevens about going through with it and he said, "There's a guy, Sidney. I play golf with him now and then. Never got married. He just has this very insular life. And he has to have everything just the way he wants it. He never lived with anybody, so he never had to compromise. And, frankly he's one big pain in the ass."

I'd like to tell you that marriage and family have prevented me from becoming an insular pain in the ass. OK, so I'm not insular. Come on. You live long enough you get set in your ways, married, single, or any weird lifestyle you choose. But kids ... kids have strong wills. And though they are too young to be set in their ways, they are strong in their ways. Of course, they pick it up from their folks. Having two strong-willed parents doesn't hurt. But along with the time ... the actual hours that it takes to bring up kids and therefore the actual hours that you spend not taking care of yourself (being insular) there is the giving up of ... space ... as we call it. You give up space. You give up ways that you would be set in if some kid didn't test you.

You do things you wouldn't do ... I don't know...ski. I'm not a skier. I look stupid going fast downhill on those two narrow pieces of plastic. And I'm afraid I'm going to die. And look stupid doing it. I do like cross-country skiing, though. It's more like sliding along in bedroom slippers ... in freezing weather. But I've often been cajoled into going out on a wintry afternoon to be with them. And I loved it. Being cajoled out of laziness keeps you alive. And allowing yourself to be cajoled is a learning experience. There is a moment, a nanosecond, when you think, "I really don't wanna get up off this couch, but I know I'll enjoy the skiing if I go, and I know it's good for me, but I really don't wanna get off this couch, but we'd all have a great time, and I'd regret missing it, but despite that, I really don't wanna get off this couch."

"We'll stop at that place for hot chocolate after."

"OK … Let's go!"

And afterwards, exhilarated, you know that, but for the insistence of your kids, you would not have gone. And it makes you more available to life. To the next time, not just one of your kids, but anyone, asks you to get up off the couch and *do* something.

Kids naturally say "yes" to stuff. And as you get older you "naturally" say "no." And you start to atrophy.

Doing stuff is what life is all about. And kids make you do it.

But here's the most important thing I learned from my kids: Giving in to them does not make you a wimp. I was never going to be a Marine-drill-sergeant parent. I'd hoped to be tougher in gentler ways. Making them clean up their room. Making them get up on time without prodding, and so forth. Okay, I failed at that. But having your way just because you're the parent is dumb. Sometimes kids know more than you do. Not life experience more. Just … life enthusiasm more.

I also like to think that this is good for them. This is a life lesson for them, this bullying you. They are learning that, to get on in life, you have to go after what you want. If it's kicking your dad out of the living room where he's enjoying a baseball game, you have to do it, because some day you'll want something more important and because it worked on Dad it can work on something really, really important. It can get you a job. Or a woman. Or a whole life, that you really, really want and that, if you had not practiced on your parents, you might be too timid to go for.

Kids grow up by testing you. They are testing your love. They are testing your patience. They are testing your knowledge ... and soaking it up. They are students and teachers. They are your biggest fans and your severest critics. They are exhausting. But now, as I sit alone in my living room, watching a Yankee game, indulging in the quiet of their absence, I miss them beyond all I ever imagined missing anything.

ACKNOWLEDGEMENTS

Thanks to Ann Treistman, editor supreme, who took a mess of memories and helped shape them into a book. Joe Pittman who picked up the baton and took it over the finish line. To my friends who read early drafts and urged me on, especially Ken and Cathy Greenwald and Martha Rush-Meuller. And to Julia Lord, whose energy and enthusiasm got it into print.

www.ingramcontent.com/pod-product-compliance
Lightning Source LLC
Chambersburg PA
CBHW031410290426
44110CB00011B/327